William Lewis Hodgson

William Hodgins, Commonwealth Avenue dining room

WILLIAM HODGINS

INTERIORS

STEPHEN M. SALNY

W.W. NORTON & COMPANY

NEW YORK • LONDON

TO ALAN SALNY,

MY LATE FATHER
WHO SO LOOKED FORWARD TO THIS BOOK.

For information about permission to reproduce selections from this book, write to Permissions, W. W. Norton & Company, Inc., 500 Fifth Avenue, New York, NY 10110

For information about special discounts for bulk purchases, please contact W. W. Norton Special Sales at specialsales@wwnorton.com or 800-233-4830

Manufacturing by KHL Printing Co. Pte Ltd
Book design by Abigail Sturges
Production manager: Leeann Graham

Library of Congress Cataloging-in-Publication Data

Salny, Stephen M.
 William Hodgins interiors / Stephen M. Salny ;
foreword by Margaret Russell. — First edition.
      pages cm
Includes bibliographical references and index.
ISBN 978-0-393-73346-4 (hardcover)
1. Hodgins, William, 1932– Themes, motives.
2. Interior decoration—United States. I. Title.
NK2004.3.H63A4 2013
747.0973—dc23

                                  2013015252

ISBN: 978-0-393-73346-4

W. W. Norton & Company, Inc.,
500 Fifth Avenue, New York, N.Y. 10110
www.wwnorton.com

W. W. Norton & Company Ltd.,
Castle House, 75/76 Wells Street, London W1T 3QT

0 9 8 7 6 5 4 3 2 1

CONTENTS

FOREWORD

When the subject of color comes up in a conversation with an interior decorator, there is always a strong chance that sparks might fly. I distinctly remember attending a dinner party about a dozen years ago with the legendary designer Albert Hadley and having the temerity to say that I was bored with neutral rooms. I said that beige is just beige and didn't really deserve to be called a color. I inadvertently struck a nerve, prompting a spirited lecture from Mr. Hadley—one that included dramatic hand gestures for emphasis. "Beige isn't beige. Beige is *atmosphere*," he announced. He then proceeded to hail a litany of neutrals, among them parchment, biscuit, toast, cappuccino, and nougat, and concluded by proclaiming that not only was beige a color, it was "simply magic."

White has a similar hold on another great decorating talent: William Hodgins, a Hadley protégé who left Parish-Hadley Associates in New York City in the late 1960s to set up his own highly influential firm in Boston—a move that led to him becoming a regular presence in the pages of *Architectural Digest* over the years. When he was named to the magazine's inaugural AD100 list of architects and interior designers in 1990, Hodgins described his work as "personal and thoughtful—it reflects the needs of my clients. It tends to be understated, quietly elegant, and especially comfortable." Though a selection of strikingly colorful rooms can be found in *William Hodgins Interiors,* Stephen Salny's marvelous book about Hodgins's long and fascinating career, it's clear that the designer is captivated by white and its myriad variations, an unexpectedly soulful range that Hodgins memorably calls "an infinity of colors between chalk and stone."

White might technically be the absence of color; however, the spaces Hodgins has fashioned are anything but empty. White can be crisp or soothing, dense or limpid, powdery or sleek, and as perfectly suited to an ultramodern interior as it is to a traditional room with a classical mien. Just as important, white means a designer has to work even harder at his or her craft. As Hodgins explains,

"In a white room there is no place to hide," so furniture and objects come into full focus, whether a gilt-wood Empire side chair in the designer's dining room in Manchester-by-the-Sea, Massachusetts, or an angular bronze-and-glass cocktail table in a client's pied-à-terre in San Francisco. When surrounded by white, every object in a room suddenly becomes as much a piece of sculpture as it is a furnishing or accessory. That's a daunting prospect, no matter how much experience you have in creating beautiful spaces.

Like Mr. Hadley's dreamy takes on beige, white in the hands of William Hodgins becomes magic. Though there is a reserved, controlled quality to his work, I also see in it a sense of grace and romance. His reductive palette isn't in the least restrictive; even a room that looks absolutely colorless at first glance is, upon closer inspection, leavened, gently, with a touch of citron silk or stone-blue velvet. And, as in the paintings of Agnes Martin and Giorgio Morandi, in Hodgins's rooms texture can provide the same impact that a bold shade might offer in another designer's hands. Consider how much visual richness and textural value is added by the dusky patina of an antique leather stool, the distressed paint of an eighteenth-century commode, the glossy lacquer of a minimalist cocktail table, or the button tufting of a Victorian-style slipper chair.

Such careful selections are evidence of Hodgins's deliberation, keen eye, and sensitivity to atmosphere, whether the project is the residence of the U.S. ambassador to France or a wing of a Saudi Arabian palace. With skills like those, it is no wonder some of the grandest names in the world—Engelhard, Rohatyn, Taubman—have commissioned Hodgins to create some of the subtlest and most intriguing interiors of our time. And as *William Hodgins Interiors* makes abundantly clear, its subject is a man whose distinguished persona and discreet rooms have, and will continue, to inspire and influence the next generations of design talent.

—Margaret Russell,
Editor in Chief, *Architectural Digest*

William Hodgins with Sam at Manchester-by-the-Sea

AN OVERVIEW

"Mr. Hodgins," as he is addressed by his devoted clients, staff, and associates alike, places first in all he does good manners and a sense of propriety. He does not accept commissions for their notoriety. Rather, his projects are the culmination of a desire to create something personal and intimate for particular people by engaging them, working with them closely, and "spending a lot of time finding out what they like" to understand "their feelings for their homes." His work rarely appears on the huge scale of other designers. He values, first and throughout, the relationship of decorator and client. All else revolves around an efficient and appropriate method of work. This decorum and harmony is why clients from all over the United States—and the world—seek William Hodgins out.

Noticeably tall, with closely trimmed graying blond hair, finely tooled wire-rimmed glasses, and conservative attire—usually punctuated by a Charvet bow tie—William Hodgins resembles nothing so much as a scholarly professor. Yet his sought-after and distinctive styling has made him one of the most talented and revered decorators in America. Hodgins's rooms are beautiful, thoughtful, and poetic. They tend to be airy, light-filled spaces. They are also as "extraordinarily luxurious as they can be in a quiet,

understated way." Handsome architectural detailing and a soothing palette work their magic and create visual flow, as if Hodgins is a master artist, painting canvases reminiscent of Merchant-Ivory imprints. A William Hodgins interior is governed by white, and the decorator is uncannily versed in the slightest subtleties and different shades of white. Yet he is also well known for his understanding and judicious use of exquisitely clear and jewel-like colors. This skillful combination of color is what makes his interiors special, inviting, and comfortable. His particular whites "reflect the quality of life and light in a room." They "glow behind the art and furniture," are restful and timeless, and age gracefully.

William Lewis Hodgins was born in Talara, Peru, in 1932 to William Lewis Hodgins Sr. and Winefred Ena Hodgins. The Hodginses hailed from the military town of London, Ontario, but William Sr., who was an engineer for the Imperial Oil Company, had been sent by Imperial to Peru to explore for oil. In 1936, Hodgins returned to Canada with his wife and sons William and Alec, who was born in 1934. William Sr. was ill on their return and died that same year.

The Great Depression in full swing, the Hodgins family evolved. Young "Bill" Hodgins excelled in school. According

Hodgins dining room, Manchester-by-the-Sea

to his Aunt Pat Barré, he also sketched from childhood, "when he always had a pencil and paper in front of him." He had "control of his hand by the first grade" and was exceptionally talented. Hodgins had always been a good worker and was "devoted to whatever he did and gave it his full attention," including the Cub Scouts. As a Cub Scout, he marched in civic and religious parades. Hodgins was also a member of the Server's Guild at St. Paul's Anglican Cathedral. In his purple gown with white cassock, Hodgins, always the tallest among his peers, marched with his fellow servers down the center aisle of the cathedral, often carrying the cross, to the high altar where they prepared the wine for Holy Communion.

Hodgins graduated with honors from high school—the London Central Collegiate Institute—in 1951. Then he entered the University of Western Ontario, where he studied General Arts—English, French, history, and the classics. He was already fluent in Spanish from his childhood days in Peru. Hodgins graduated from the university in 1954 with a bachelor of arts.

After graduation, Hodgins set out to hitchhike throughout Europe. He had a propensity for knowledge and learning and wanted to visit places where he had never been before. His journey began in Montreal, where he boarded a small freighter bound for England. Initially, he settled in Hampstead, in the London borough of Camden, where he rented a room in a "big grand house." The twelve-bedroom house was occupied mostly by English youth from situations similar to Hodgins's. They lived communally and with great camaraderie, including mealtime when they all cooked together.

While living in London, Hodgins worked in Sloane Square at Peter Jones—one of the largest and best-known department stores in the city. He worked in the store's "ironmongery" department. When first hired, Hodgins did not understand this designation to mean hardware and housewares, but he adjusted. He sold pots and pans and hand-crank food mixers for four months. While working at Peter Jones, Hodgins made the acquaintance of Lady Verney, "a short little gal wearing a toque like Queen Mary" who became a good customer of Hodgins's because cooking was her hobby. She soon invited Hodgins for tea at the Verney home. In time, Lady Verney and Hodgins became close friends and she and her husband, Sir Ralph Verney, despaired of Hodgins's position in a department store, no matter how well known, and suggested to him that he "do something more suitable." Sir Ralph, who was well connected in London, recommended Hodgins for the position of "gopher" at the Commonwealth Parliamentary Association, an organization of parliamentarians from throughout the Commonwealth. Major Lockhart, the

director of the association, hired Hodgins for the post, and for the next ten months Hodgins attended to the various needs of MPs from around the world as well as serving members of the British government.

His allotted year in Britain at an end, Hodgins's next stop on his sojourn was Paris. Here, he rented a bedroom that lay within a warren of staff rooms in the eaves of an old apartment building. The room came with nothing more for furniture than a single bed and chest of drawers. Hodgins remembers how cramped the quarters were, with hardly a foot of space between the edge of his bed and the wall. In fact, because the ceiling was so low, he could "barely get into [the room]." Nonetheless, the room was affordable.

Hodgins found work at the grocery department in the basement of the American Embassy. He was one of several box boys who carried groceries for customers. His salary was "nothing," but the American ladies tipped very well. At least Hodgins and his coworkers, most who hailed from South Africa, got their food at cost. Between his deliveries to some of the finest residences in Paris, and his wanderings when not at work but unable to bare the closeness of his quarters, Hodgins saw much of the city.

After this year in Paris, in 1956, Hodgins returned to Canada. Following his long period away, he felt the need to be closer to his widowed mother. He soon took a job at the Hudson Bay Company, which had a good retail training program. To begin, Hodgins traveled by rail with his fellow trainees to Edmonton, where the Bay conducted a three-month course. When Hodgins completed the program, he was assigned to the ladies' and children's shoe department at a Hudson Bay store in Edmonton. Hodgins preferred to work in the men's clothing department, but the Bay's management preached to their employees "how lucky they were to have a job." No one properly questioned his assignment. Hodgins stayed with it for a while, but it was hopeless. He resigned his position.

Next, Hodgins landed a good position with Avon, the international cosmetics and perfume company, at their headquarters in Montreal. He worked in sales promotion, where he helped produce a new brochure every three weeks for Avon saleswomen. The job paid well. It also opened his eyes to the possibilities of design. Whether it was creating a brochure or rearranging the furniture in his family home when he was growing up, even though "it drove [his] mother crazy [as] she never knew where things were going to be when she came home from work," Hodgins "always liked making things look better and appealing." He had a longstanding "fascination" with becoming a decorator, and the position with Avon gave him the time to think about what he wanted to do, especially since he "came to the conclusion that you spend half of your conscious life at work so you better like it." So, in 1961, Hodgins resigned from Avon and applied to design school.

His choice was the Parsons School of Design in New York. It was the foremost school for interior design and fashion in the United States. The school required him to prepare a portfolio of sketches as part of the admissions process. Hodgins was prepared. He made good use of his childhood talent and the one-year extracurricular art course he took at the H. B. Beal Technical School in London, Ontario, during high school. Hodgins submitted several sketches in charcoal and pencil, as well as a few watercolors, to Parsons. They were all imagined interiors, products of many years of thinking. Parsons accepted him. The tuition was $800 a year.

The curriculum at Parsons for first-year students included Freehand Drawing and Painting, Basic Interior Design Problems, and Presentation Techniques. Stanley Barrows, the preeminent director of the school's interior design department from 1946 to 1968 and a recognized authority on period history and design, was head of the second-year program. He taught Hodgins and his classmates, as well as many of America's leading decorators, the history of interior design from the seventeenth to the twentieth centuries. Students also learned about antiques and period rooms in the classroom and during their engaging field trips to the Metropolitan Museum of Art. It was during Hodgins's third and final year at Parsons that Barrows helped him acquire a part-time job with Rose Cumming, the "flamboyant and exotic" Park Avenue decorator whose clients included Mary Pickford, Marlene Dietrich, and Gloria Swanson. Cumming, at Barrows's recommendation, gave Hodgins "an interview of sorts" and "told him to come in the next day." Hodgins worked as her "gopher" several days a week after school and all day on Saturdays. Cumming, who "liked young men," asked Hodgins to "tag along for lunch once in awhile because he was tall, and spoke good English." He, in turn, "loved her shop," which was filled with wonderful treasures.

As a third-year student at Parsons, Hodgins was required to complete a class project commensurate with a real-life commission. He began the assignment by wandering through the various antique, design, and decoration shops that were located in the same building as Parsons on East Fifty-Fourth Street at Sutton Place. He was inspired by the array of unique and outstanding compilations that he saw in the shops and by their proprietors who welcomed him and his fellow classmates. Finally, Hodgins settled for his project on a plan to decorate a three-floor townhouse. With the help of a friend, he ingeniously divided the interior into three distinct venues: a one-floor apartment, a duplex

Scheft living room

apartment, and a studio apartment in the basement. Each arrangement, which favored classic and traditional design, was skillfully composed. His instructors praised Hodgins for his resourceful and superlative work. During his three years at Parsons, he had effectively balanced the rigorous and demanding agenda of the school along with his need to work part-time. Hodgins graduated cum laude from Parsons, the oldest student in a graduating class of 132. The news made his mother "proud and pleased" even though initially "she didn't understand why he would leave a good job to attend Parsons."

Hodgins began his post-Parsons life with an apprenticeship on a full-time basis with Michael Greer. Greer was a prominent Upper East Side decorator who was also an alumnus of Parsons and then at the pinnacle of his career. Greer hired Hodgins to be his "junior-junior assistant" and, although Hodgins would remain with Greer for eighteen months, he never came to care for Greer's formulaic style, which Hodgins found expensive but not lush. However, Hodgins credits Greer for teaching him the business aspects of decorating, including "how to make

Scheft library

the darkly stained wood floor, which was interspersed with palm matting and underscored Hadley's collection of white plaster furniture, including a chic dolphin-based console table designed by Syrie Maugham, the renowned English decorator. But most impressive in the room by far was the presence of Mrs. Parish.

The air in the room was one of extreme formality. Hodgins was nervous and overawed during the thirty minutes that Hadley and Sister Parish interviewed him. They inquired about his practical experience, including his abilities at drafting, going so far as to ask him to sketch floor plans as they talked. They also wanted to know if he was experienced at shopping for materials. Although Hodgins felt that the interview went well, he really had no idea of his standing when he left the apartment. It was not until the following day that Hadley called him and said, simply, "You're hired."

Hodgins arrived at Parish-Hadley in the fall of 1964, just as the partnership was evolving from a small, casually run firm with one assistant—Edward Lee Cave—who later founded the well-known New York real estate company bearing his name, and a minimal office staff, into the formidable organization it became. Although Hodgins was technically the assistant to Mrs. Parish, both "Madam"—Hodgins's nickname for Mrs. Parish—and "Mr. Hadley" mentored him. Hodgins remembers them as "teachers, respected friends, and cohorts" who taught him "everything—scale, color, integrity," and that "a room must be usable first, then it will always be inviting." They cared deeply about their clients, which made a lasting impression on Hodgins. He also attained a degree of self-assurance while working in an environment of almost unimaginable privilege. The list of extraordinary clients included Charles Engelhard, the international mines and metals industrialist; his wife Jane Engelhard; William Paley, the chairman of CBS; his wife Barbara (Babe) Paley; and Ambassador John (Jock) Hay Whitney, the sportsman, investor, and publisher, and his wife Betsey Whitney.

Although Hodgins was very happy during the nearly five years he worked at Parish-Hadley, he finally did not want to live in New York City any longer. He found New York to be "too city, too big, too large, too everything." Hodgins had grown up in a "sleepy university town" whose population was 120,000 people. Boston's "wonderful size" and close proximity to New York appealed to him. Hodgins had many friends there—people he had met both in New York and in Provincetown, where he had worked as "a very good bartender and an equally good waiter" during the summers following his first and second years at Parsons. Hodgins had also visited Boston regularly

estimates and do curtain treatments." Greer, in 1964, also gave Hodgins an "unqualified recommendation" for membership in the American Institute of Interior Designers (AID), the first national professional organization for interior designers in the United States. He was admitted that same year.

At the time, Billy Baldwin, Sister Parish, and her partner Albert Hadley were the three "quintessential" American decorators. Hodgins aspired to work for either Baldwin or the Parish-Hadley office, and again he turned to his mentor, Stanley Barrows. Barrows "pushed" Hodgins to ask Albert Hadley if "by chance" Parish-Hadley had an opening. Barrows also recommended Hodgins to Hadley. Hadley, who always "paid close attention to Stanley," in turn asked Hodgins to meet with him and Sister Parish.

The interview was held at Hadley's "quietly dazzling" apartment on East Seventy-Fourth Street, five blocks from the Parish-Hadley office. Hodgins "had never seen anything like Hadley's living room." It was "very simple," but glamorous at the same time. The walls were covered in silver, antiqued tea paper "of a beautiful [soft] quality" and with "seams that you could see." Hodgins also admired on weekends when he was living in New York. And, fortunately, a good job was waiting for him there.

Benjamin Cook was the founder and principal of Trade Winds, Boston's esteemed and nationally known interior decorating firm. Cook learned through Kevin McNamara, his good friend and a Parish-Hadley assistant whose tenure at the firm overlapped slightly with Hodgins's, that Hodgins was relocating to the city. On hearing the news, Cook visited New York, invited Hodgins to lunch, and offered him a job as an assistant decorator. Hodgins accepted.

Enchanted with the architecture of Beacon Hill, Hodgins chose the historic neighborhood as the place where he wanted to live. However, much to his chagrin, he soon found that he was not the only one, and that the rents in the legendary Boston neighborhood were as costly as New York. He settled for a room at the Harvard Club, sponsored by Norman and Eleanor Rabb, clients of Mrs. Parish's. Mrs. Rabb also helped launch Hodgins in Boston, graciously allowing him to show her stylish apartment to prospective clients as he was the assistant to Sister Parish when she decorated the Rabbs' Back Bay penthouse.

Hodgins lived at the Harvard Club for three months. The apartment that he finally settled on, while not on Beacon Hill, was close enough, in Back Bay at 191 Commonwealth Avenue. The Hotel Agassiz, named in honor of the family who built it in 1872, was considered the Dakota of Boston. The very proper and foreboding dark-brown brick building shared clean Victorian details, towering bays, and French flats with its considerably grander New York counterpart. A smallish apartment that had been carved out of the second floor and overlooked Commonwealth Avenue became Hodgins's new home. Trade Winds, which was located at 141 Newbury Street, was only a few blocks away.

At Trade Winds, Hodgins established himself professionally in Boston while also developing loyal relationships with his clients. At first, Cook sent Hodgins out as "the young man who just came from New York" to work on jobs. By October of 1969, however, it was clear that Hodgins was a successful designer in his own right. He left Trade Winds, carrying overflow clients and a strong desire to be on his own. He called his firm William Hodgins Incorporated and worked out of his Commonwealth Avenue apartment, which he decorated with sun-yellow textured walls and white canvas slipcovered furniture. Hodgins hired a secretary, Carol Stahl, and established her in the nice hall in front. At the end of the day he would put her typewriter under the desk.

His first major coup came in 1970 when he met Julian Cohen, the Boston real estate developer, and his wife Eunice Cohen. Hodgins recalled that "working on an apartment for them was one of my first jobs when I moved

Scheft master bedroom

to Boston. I had just started out on my own, I had virtually no clients, and I was referred by [Ben Cook] to work on one of their bedrooms because the job was too small for him." Mr. and Mrs. Cohen immediately recognized Hodgins's singular talent with their initial commission and "seized upon this classic American decorator who trained in New York." Their "wonderfully supportive encouragement" and generous patronage of Hodgins endured for many decades.

Another major breakthrough came with a commission for Bill and Gitty Scheft, for whom Hodgins had worked during his first few months at Trade Winds. The parents of six children, Mr. and Mrs. Scheft had recently purchased a large Victorian in Beverly Farms, Massachusetts, overlooking the Atlantic Ocean. They wanted to convert the property into a summer place for themselves and their children. The house showed much promise from the outside, but it had been purchased from an elderly woman in poor health who had allowed it to sink into appalling condition. As gloomy and forlorn as its interiors were, Hodgins knew that he could rejuvenate it. In fact, so confident was Hodgins in the potential of his design, he

Junior League Decorators' Show
House 1971, master bedroom

predicted at the beginning of the project, when the place was at its worst, that the Schefts would come to love it so much, they would make it their permanent home.

Hodgins created an informal and comfortable home for the Schefts. He lightened the interiors with bright colors and materials and combined furnishings of old and new, including wicker from "all kinds of dilapidated shops in New York." The final project was featured in the January 1971 issue of *House Beautiful* magazine. Even the Scheft children loved Hodgins's metamorphosis, especially their bedrooms "where he gave them what they wanted—with taste!" After their first summer in the house, the Scheft family validated Hodgins's magical transformation—and his powers of prophecy—even further. They moved to the Beverly Farms house permanently.

William Hodgins Incorporated outgrew its home office by the winter of 1971 and moved to 133 Newbury Street, four doors away from Trade Winds. The new decorating office included a shop, which displayed shelves of wonderful treasures for sale, including accessories, lamps, and bibelots that Hodgins gathered during his extensive travels, especially from London, England. Penny Matteson started at the firm shortly after the move to Newbury Street. Although Matteson began her job answering

the telephone, running errands, and walking Hodgins's dogs, she gradually but fairly quickly began working on small projects with Hodgins, before work and after hours. Within two years Penny Matteson became an assistant designer at the firm. Today, she is an established senior designer with Hodgins and the longest-standing member of his staff.

Though just beginning to build his business himself, Hodgins took the time and showed the patience to mentor many of his early employees in the way he had been mentored at Parish-Hadley. Every Monday, during office hours, Hodgins gave a hypothetical project to his employees, profiling the clients and the parameters of the commission. Hodgins required his employees to complete the assignments on their own time. Fortunately, Matteson and her handful of coworkers had the office sample room at their disposal. They also benefited from Hodgins's committed ability to bring out the potential in his staff and his weekly critiques of the finished projects, which he did with them—after hours. Hodgins has always been a "strict taskmaster" with very high standards for himself and his staff, and has launched many of their careers.

In the spring of 1971 the Junior League of Boston heralded Hodgins by including him in their first Decorators' Show House in Massachusetts. Hodgins, along with forty-six Boston-area decorators, refurbished the Bancroft Davis House—a late-nineteenth-century shingle-style Queen Anne and its carriage house in the town of Weston, which lies fourteen miles west of Boston. Hodgins decorated the master bedroom and bathroom. The bedroom was "a quiet retreat, lined and upholstered in Swiss linen—highlighted with soft silk and madras, a background for a very personal collection of furniture and objects." The bathroom was "large, crisp, and soft with carpets and ribbons." The bedroom suite served as an effective calling card for Hodgins. It attracted new clients, including Carol Feinberg. Mrs. Feinberg and her husband, Norman Feinberg, became "hooked on Hodgins" from the moment they saw his work. Forty years later, Mrs. Feinberg, now Carol Cohen, remains a loyal and devoted client of Hodgins's. *House & Garden* magazine photographed the Weston bedroom and featured it one year later in the double-page spread "How to Make Your Dreams Work for You." Dr. Ann Faraday, a psychologist and author of book, Dream Power, wrote the accompanying piece. Hodgins's bedroom, with its "serene colors" according to Dr. Faraday's book, which offered "insight into your sleeping life," prompted "serene dreams." The heightened coverage further endorsed and advanced Hodgins's career.

The Junior League of Boston welcomed Hodgins again when they hosted their second annual Decorators' Show

Junior League Decorators' Show House
1972, first-floor sitting room

Berenson living room

232 Clarendon Street

House during the spring of 1972. That year the venue was the historic Edwin S. Webster House in Chestnut Hill. Hodgins decorated the first-floor sitting room of the Colonial Revival house. His surprising choice was "comfortable modern furniture, romantic antiques, and modern art." Again, *House & Garden* featured Hodgins's work. The September 1972 article, "Introducing 6 New H & G Colors," featured the show house sitting room, with its dark gloss "sweet chocolate" walls. The piece also displayed a living room bathed in "shell" white. It was a room that Hodgins decorated for Teddy and Eleanor Berenson, another Boston-area couple who had become enamored of Hodgins's new "marvelously versatile" colors.

William Hodgins Incorporated continued to flourish during the early 1970s, and the business relocated again in the summer of 1973. Hodgins's monthly rent on Newbury Street had also climbed to the then-astronomical amount of $650. Always equipped with a keen eye for real estate, Hodgins found a landmark Victorian townhouse nearby, at 232 Clarendon Street. The house, of course, had a story. Lydia Pinkham, one of America's nineteenth-century patent medicine queens—she of the "Pink Pills for Pale People" regimen—built the red brick townhouse in 1872. The building had been vacant for nearly thirty

Hope House bedroom, 1976

years when Hodgins discovered it on one of his custom-ary strolls through the neighborhood. Hodgins purchased and gradually renovated the four-story building from its deplorable condition. At first, his design office occupied the building's first floor and basement. He leased the second floor to Sotheby Parke Bernet, the art auctioneers and appraisers, for their first public office in Boston, and the third and fourth floors became his new home.

By the time Hodgins moved to Clarendon Street, he was already the leading interior decorator in Boston. His professional advice and expertise were in great demand. In 1976, the American Society of Interior Designers (ASID)—following the 1975 merger of AID and the National Society of Interior Designers—invited him and twenty-six other members to each decorate a room in the twenty-seven-room manor house at the Cabot Estate overlooking Jamaica Pond in Brookline, Massachusetts. The occasion was Hope House, a benefit held collectively for the Sidney Farber Cancer Institute in Boston and the New England chapter of the American Cancer Society. Hodgins chose and deco-rated a small, unprepossessing back bedroom in the historic

English-style stone house. Joan Daniels, a longstanding cli-ent and friend of Hodgins's and a chairperson of the Hope House project, said that Hodgins "magically transformed" the ordinary and awkward garret bedroom into a comfort-able, engaging, and visually spacious interior. He arranged the dormered room with a balanced mélange of antiques, contemporary furniture, and eclectic accessories. He deployed his signature palette of lush and restrained white, cream, and pale blue. The outstanding bedroom, with its continuous aroma of fresh pine, drew a long line of attend-ees every day during the month-long event.

As Hodgins's business grew, his commissions, which originally were concentrated in New England, broadened to other locales, including New York, Florida, and the Virginia Hunt Country. In New York, Felix and Elizabeth Rohatyn hired him to decorate their Georgian-style duplex apartment on Park Avenue. They also commissioned him in later years to decorate a second apartment in New York, houses in Southampton (New York) and Wyoming, and the private quarters in the American ambassador's resi-dence in Paris when President Clinton appointed Felix

Rohatyn the U.S. Ambassador to France in 1997. They have been clients of Hodgins's for over thirty years.

Sophie Engelhard, whose mother, Jane Engelhard, was a great friend and patron of Hodgins's from his days at Parish-Hadley, hired him to renovate and decorate the informal Colonial-style house she purchased during the late 1970s in Hume, Virginia. The house, which faced soft rolling hills and, in the distance, the outline of the Blue Ridge Mountains, was Hodgins's second commission for Engelhard. Her mother "found Bill" for her and her sister Charlene Engelhard when they were at school in Boston. Hodgins decorated apartments for both Charlene and Sophie Engelhard during the mid-1970s when they attended graduate school at Harvard. He has also decorated innumerable houses for Charlene, Sophie, and their sister Sally Pingree through the years.

In January 1981, Paige Rense, then the editor in chief of *Architectural Digest*, introduced Hodgins to the magazine's readership. In her editorial, "People Are the Issue," Rense wrote of Hodgins, wondering "why more interior designers and architects don't come to our attention in Boston; it is a city with so much inherent taste and character." She was "pleased to be showing the work of William Hodgins" for the first time. The commission featured in that issue of the magazine was one for Charlene Engelhard in Cambridge, Massachusetts. Engelhard had hired Hodgins to decorate a mid-nineteenth-century farmhouse not far from the duplex apartment that he did for her in 1974. The white clapboard house, which had originally been surrounded by a lot of land, emanated "New England Charm." Hodgins's "aim was to create a personal ambience: romantic, but lightly so."

In the two-level living room, Hodgins added a cornice and paneling, which Lewis F. Perry's Sons glazed darkly in aubergine, creating an effective background for a distinctive collection of antiques, including a French settee, a birthing chair, and seventeenth-century English crewel-work curtains. Upholstery in silk, velvet, and taffeta enhanced the opulence and "old-world decorations" without diminishing its requisite degree of comfort.

The relationship of the house to nature contributed casualness and beautiful light to its interior. In the dining room, Robert Jackson, the New York muralist and master of trompe-l'oeil artistry, painted cascading leaves on the walls and cornice to create "a light-hearted mood." The glassed-in garden room located at the back of the house, but clearly visible from the entrance hall, a large window of mullioned glass in the living room, and adjacent dining room, also integrated the indoors with the New England landscape.

Hodgins created a romantic master bedroom/sitting

Engelhard living room, Cambridge

Engelhard dining room, Cambridge

Engelhard master bedroom, Cambridge

room for Engelhard. He combined two small rooms into one, heightened the interior with a tray ceiling, and had Robert Jackson paint the cornice with a recurring pattern of swags and bows. "Gray Roses" wallpaper from Brunschwig & Fils and the "special" mauve-and-blue-on-white chintz bedspread covering the antique German bed highlighted the charming setting.

Architectural Digest continued its coverage of Hodgins when the magazine featured his commission for Mr. and Mrs. Taylor Chewning on the cover of the September 1981 issue. This time, however, rather than being "introduced" by the magazine, Paige Rense telegrammed Hodgins to tell him that he had made the cover. "Rock Cliff," the Chewning house in Newport, Rhode Island, had once belonged to Harold S. Vanderbilt, the renowned yachtsman and American railroad executive. Originally a simple half-timbered seaside cottage, during the early 1900s the house had been dramatically enlarged, covered in stucco, and remodeled in the style of Louis XVI.

The *AD* cover featured Taylor and Mary Chewning's library, with its geometric-patterned carpet, dark wool upholstery, and strié walls glazed by Lewis F. Perry's Sons, all in deep shades of emerald green. Although Hodgins's decoration of the library was certainly current and dramatic, it was the only room in the house where he maintained a traditional color scheme. Because, although the Chewnings relished the library, they "wanted a bright atmosphere" throughout the rest of the house. In other words, a Hodgins décor. Hodgins chose a palette of soft colors, which lent "a contemporary feeling to a design that [fit] a delightfully old-fashioned way of living" that the house stood for. However, the look of the house was never "period" or "stiffly formal."

The refreshing quality of Hodgins's décor was especially apparent in the spacious living room, where he arranged the furniture, both antique and classic contemporary, on either side of a skirted round table to create two large sitting areas and an illusion of intimacy. Floral-patterned yellow chintz from Brunschwig & Fils covered the oversized sofas and chairs. Curtains fabricated in sky-blue linen harmonized with the walls, which were strié and glazed in the "palest mauve" and the view of the ocean, contributing casualness to an interior that was originally heavy and somber.

Hodgins complemented the living room's color palette in the connecting sunroom where he upholstered a suite of antique wicker furniture in vibrant green canvas printed by Leslie Tillett and D. D. Tillett, the "visionary husband-and-wife textile designers" of postwar American design. Alternate designs of white trellis, which were interspersed with dots and sprays of white and yellow Queen Anne's lace,

ARCHITECTURAL DIGEST

THE INTERNATIONAL MAGAZINE OF FINE INTERIOR DESIGN   SEPTEMBER 1981 $4.00

Chewning library,
Newport

decorated the material, advancing the room's relationship with the outdoors and its dramatic view of the ocean. The glazed-tile floor and tile-topped coffee table were appropriate to the informal and practical interior.

The dining room, detailed with a handcrafted period cornice, moldings, and pilasters, was the most traditional room in the house. Here, Hodgins offset rare antiques—a Duncan Phyfe mahogany dining table, eighteenth-century American shield-back chairs, and a nineteenth-century American crystal chandelier that came from the governor's mansion in Pennsylvania, against soft hues, including curtains of unlined and restrained mauve silk taffeta

that puddled on the floor and billowed against the ocean breeze. As the *AD* cover suggested, the effect was dramatic, and the prominent coverage introduced Hodgins's work beyond New England.

Hodgins created his own weekend retreat in 1985 when he purchased a carriage house on Boston's North Shore in Manchester-by-the-Sea. The secluded late-nineteenth-century dependency, which originally belonged to a neighboring estate house, was distinguished by a quirkiness that appealed to Hodgins. He was drawn to its "odd, slightly off-center peaked turret and weathered shingles." He felt as if the structure was "one of those whimsical English garden

19

Chewning living room, Newport

Chewning sunroom, Newport

Chewning living room, Newport

Chewning dining room, Newport

structures known as follies, mysteriously washed up on the Massachusetts shore." Hodgins had "never been so taken with a place." The two-story carriage house, which faced Lobster Cove, required considerable renovation. Originally converted into a residence in the 1930s, to restore it Hodgins's tasks included raising the first-floor ceilings to their original height of 9'8", adding period architectural details, and orienting the house toward the quiet saltwater cove by installing three sets of wide French doors on the garden side. The new doors opened from the living room and the adjacent master bedroom onto a large new deck stained gray to match the shingles.

Hodgins, with his love of gardening, also created a pot garden on the deck, bordered an existing stone wall with flowers, and placed a cutting garden and flower beds all in sight of the interiors of the carriage house. Inside he enveloped the interiors with his favorite palette—"an infinity of colors between chalk and stone." The non-colors spoke of Hodgins's classic style and the importance of subtleties in his work, which allow the eye to "focus on forms" of the furniture and accessories, because "in a white room there is no place to hide." Perhaps in a reference to his first apartment at the Agassiz, Hodgins redesigned the shuttered entrance hall to double as a dining room, with chalk-white walls, off-white woodwork, and pine floors. Franklin Tartaglione, the fine decorative painter, produced the checkerboard patterned floor in off-white and pale gray. John Anderson, also a talented decorative artist in Hodgins's circle, painted the late-nineteenth-century pine dining table in faux marbre, its shades of cream and pale gray sustaining Hodgins's palette of "old-world white." For Hodgins's office and its craftsmen, this color was "shorthand not only for creamy, soft, old-looking color," but also represented for them "a state of mind."

Hodgins was drawn to the oddly shaped rooms of the carriage house. In the living room, where no two walls ran parallel, he covered them in rough linen that he then painted off-white. The "very subtle textured surface" of the walls kept the room "from looking too pristine, too antiseptic." The shape of the living room also contributed uniqueness to Hodgins's arrangement of furniture, starting with the principal wall, where a sofa upholstered in natural linen offset an antique Italian console and an ornate regency end table. The console, which Hodgins placed deftly against an angled wall, between the sofa and the fireplace, amplified with its presence the characteristic oddities of the room. Hodgins's comprehensive plan for the living room included an old repainted desk that he oriented toward the fireplace, at the foot of a light-filled corner on the opposite side of the room. Here, a generous exposure to the outdoors and the lovingly tended gardens infused restrained touches of color throughout the natural-hued interiors.

The carriage house became famous in its own right. During the 1980s and the 1990s, the house was featured in *House & Garden*, the *New York Times Magazine*, and *House Beautiful*. *SPAZIOCASA*, the Italian lifestyle magazine, also praised Hodgins and his private retreat. The article, entitled "The Quiet Charm of Classic," acknowledged him as "the master of the pale, neutral palette."

Neither were Hodgins's other projects out of the news. *Vogue* revered Hodgins in November 1986 with its feature

Hodgins dining room, Manchester-by-the-Sea
(above and opposite)

of his first commission for Robert Taubman, the real estate developer, and his wife, Linda. Linda Taubman was a native Bostonian. She knew Hodgins's superlative work by reputation and through a good friend of her mother's who was a client of his. When it came time to decorate her Michigan home, she knew exactly where to turn. Although the Taubmans' 1950s country French house had a good layout and lots of space and natural light, it was "unbelievably shabby and depressing—brightly colored, the foyer dotted with crystal chandeliers, the whole thing lacking coherence" when they bought it in 1981. As always, Hodgins, architecturally gifted, had no difficulty discerning the soul of the house. As with the Scheft project, he saw what the house

Hodgins living room,
Manchester-by-the-Sea

Hodgins living room, Manchester-by-the-Sea

might become. Single-handedly he created the charm, elegance, timelessness, and pedigreed architecture of the Taubmans' house. "He ripped out tons of unattractive marble and replaced it with much softer, more elegant stone. He then added mullions, baseboards, cornices, wainscoting, French doors, fireplaces, and wood floors to all three of its floors. He also enhanced the front of the house with a new foyer that had stylish high round windows and turned the [unfortunate] looking basement into a [handsome] theatre, billiards room, wine cellar, and exercise suite."

Hodgins furnished the house, starting from scratch. He and his clients shopped for antiques together in London, Paris, and New York where "he [has always spent] an occasional Monday through Wednesday, scouting for pieces he thinks will appeal to his clients, and then takes them to see his pre-selections on Thursday." In London, Hodgins's shopping trips with the Taubmans "ran the gamut, from Mallett on New Bond Street to Portobello Road." They also went to a great Christie's house sale in Kent, at Godmersham Park.

Taubman entrance hall, Michigan

Taubman studio, Michigan

Hodgins's well-organized shopping trips are legendary and a treat for his clients. While shopping, he mentors them judiciously and with great integrity about art and furniture. Hodgins shares with his clients the reason he choses a particular piece of furniture, explaining its characteristics patiently and in great detail, including its assemblage or the type of wood it was made from. He wants his clients to recognize quality and to be educated about their acquisitions.

Hodgins also encourages his clients to "think carefully about each piece of furniture," where it will be placed

Taubman living room, Michigan

and "how it could be used," thereby teaching them the way their homes might function—both on a day-to-day basis and for the purposes of entertaining. He makes his clients aware of how "they want to live" in their homes, often grooming them for "a different way of life." Hodgins accomplishes his mission in an old-world, gentlemanly manner. He is "never condescending" and always makes his clients "feel comfortable. That's part of who he is."

Hodgins and the Taubmans decorated the house in a soft and beautiful palette. The restraint and "serenity" of the design was unexpected and extremely ahead of its time, especially for a big traditional house. The interiors, which were "a variation on white," were neither "fancy," "fussy," nor "stuffy." The subdued background brought everything—the art, furniture, and accessories—to life.

In the entrance hall, a freestanding staircase swept before a large window of mullioned glass and trompe-l'oeil walls of stone blocks in white. Painted by Robert Jackson, the walls dramatized Hodgins's relaxed placement of antiques. There was a regency hall chair, a nineteenth-century empire painted oval table supported by intricately carved gilded swans, and a patinated plaster bust of Voltaire displayed on a sienna marble pedestal. Though the objects represented "disparate styles and periods," they harmonized flawlessly.

Distinctive antiques set against a "calm" and uncomplicated backdrop characterized the living room and "studio," so named by Hodgins because Laura Shatz—Linda Taubman's sister—painted in the room when she lived with her sister and brother-in-law. The studio opened onto an expansive bluestone terrace overlooking the Taubmans' walled formal English gardens and was filled with natural light.

They arranged the studio with unconventional antiques. Hodgins anchored the seating area by the fireplace with an ornately carved eighteenth-century Italian giltwood low table and a pair of whimsical continental empire-style painted fauteuils. Hodgins also hung a fanciful topiary chandelier above a large round stone table at the far end of the room. The chandelier and table, along with its four oversized chairs, a pair of eighteenth-century Italian Louis XVI carved walnut fauteuils and two modern reproductions, contributed rusticity to the setting.

Together, the Taubmans and Hodgins also infused spareness and serenity in the living room. Hodgins painted the walls and woodwork in his usual shades of white. He bleached the wood floors and dressed the windows with finely profiled straw blinds and cream curtains of unlined Brunschwig & Fils silk taffeta. The principal wall, which was composed of floor-to-ceiling mullioned windows overlooking the terrace, formed a spacious and welcoming bay. Here, Hodgins arranged the main seating area, anchoring it with a flat Bessarabian rug woven in a design of diamond latticework and cabbage roses in shades of green, pink, cream, and brown. He placed the sofa, which was upholstered in Scalamandré antique white damask, before the curvature of the wall and near the fireplace. He completed the seating area with a tufted slipper chair covered in Scalamandré creamy white woven textured silk, paired with an antique gueridon and a Plexiglas waterfall coffee table, whose transparency allowed the muted colors of the rug to subtly permeate the room.

Another sitting area across from the bay featured an oversized sofa, also upholstered in creamy white woven textured silk, offsetting a Louis XV painted beechwood bergère and an unusual continental ivory, glass, and Lucite low table. Mrs. Taubman's "particular weakness" for chairs informed Hodgins's choices. Four eighteenth-century Louis XVI carved giltwood oval-back fauteuils sumptuously upholstered in Brunschwig & Fils blue velvet and interspersed throughout the living room embodied her passion, independent mind, and special editing of the interiors in her house—"all which taught Hodgins a lot." "Slightly offbeat, unusual chairs can add a lot of [style] to a room without furnishing it too much."

Hodgins's prominence as an American decorator intensified in December 1987 when he was inducted into *Interior Design* magazine's Interior Design Hall of Fame. The magazine established the award in 1985 "to honor outstanding designers working in the field." Hodgins was feted, along with ten residential and contract interior designers, at the third annual awards gala, which was held at the Waldorf-Astoria Hotel in New York. Many good friends and clients, including Alvin and Helaine Allen, Stanton and Patricia Black, Austin and Marcia Cable, Lee and Joan Daniels, Carol Feinberg, and Felix and Elizabeth Rohatyn, accompanied him to the celebratory dinner. High admiration for Hodgins's decorating continued when *House & Garden* included him in "A Directory of Decorators: The best of American interior design—from New York to the Far West" published in the September 1988 issue.

Hodgins's talent, selfless and "generous outreach," and "very early efforts" on behalf of the AIDS crisis played a special role in 1988 when Charles Spada, allied member, ASID, and a well-respected interior designer in Boston, asked him to cochair the decorating committee for the AIDS Hospice at Mission Hill—the architecturally landmarked neighborhood in Roxbury, Massachusetts. The pioneering hospice, initiated by Hospice West, Inc., in Massachusetts and Spada, which was the first in the United States to be Medicare-certified specifically for AIDS, would be located in a three-story double brownstone.

Hodgins accepted Spada's appeal and "the two hit the telephones." All thirty-five assignments required to decorate the hospice were filled. Everyone wanted to participate.

The assignments included decorating sixteen small bedrooms, a lounge, a reception room, and two counseling rooms, one of which was decorated by Hodgins himself. Spada and Hodgins also asked each interior designer to bring in a scheme board outlining their plans, all following stringent hospital codes, for their particular project. The cochairmen oversaw every room to ensure continuity and devised a list of nine design guidelines based on their own experiences with dying friends. The specifications included that "colors must be upbeat, but soft, the design not complicate hospice work, create additional chores," nor bring staff, support people, or family and friends "down to the depths of institutional atmospheres."

Although the Hospice at Mission Hill had raised nearly $600,000 in addition to Hospice West's $500,000 purchase price of the brownstones, the organization depended significantly on donated and discounted products and services. Fortunately, vendors and suppliers at the Boston Design Center contributed generously to the project, including Blanche P. Field, the custom lampshade and light-

Rohatyn living room, Paris

ing products company, and Dalia Kitchen Design, which donated the entire kitchen for the hospice. Brigham and Women's Hospital in Boston contributed all of the hospital beds needed. Design volunteers painted the bed frames beige to blend in with the décor and soften their appearance.

The bedrooms had to be attractive but practical. Although bedskirts were not allowed (impractical), the interior designers often "dressed up" the beds with headboards that they attached to the wall and detailed with decorative molding. Ceiling art also uplifted several of the bedrooms—easy for a resident to look at—and decorative artists faux-painted the walls in pleasing patterns and textures that included strié and flocking.

Interior Design and *Design Times*, a New England publication, simultaneously lauded Spada and Hodgins and

their committed team of interior designers, artists, and benefactors. The illustrated March 1990 articles, respectively titled "AIDS Hospice" and "Designing from the HEART," profiled the hospice and several of its decorated rooms, including the bedroom that Paul Lanoix of William Hodgins Incorporated designed. The magazine coverage also praised the exceptional camaraderie and openness among the designers and artisans who usually "keep their doors shut" and their sources to themselves while working on a designer show house. Together and unconditionally, they created "a better quality of life for the people who would be using the space."

During the summer of 1990, *Architectural Digest*, which had already featured Hodgins's work in a dozen issues since 1981, including three covers, named him in

Rohatyn main dining room, Paris

Rohatyn small dining room, Paris

Rohatyn living room, Paris

The AD 100, its inaugural and groundbreaking directory of the finest 100 interior designers in the world. The "unparalleled" resource included "photographic examples of the designers' work, descriptions of their design principles and procedures, and practical data concerning their staffs and fee structures."

Town & Country recognized Hodgins in its November 1990 issue with its Interior Design Directory of America's finest. The comprehensive list of decorators began with the "Dazzling Dozen (the top of the top)," which included Hodgins.

Traditional Home hailed Hodgins as "a true maestro of impressionistic color and light" when it featured his Nantucket commission for Peter and Kay Bernon on the cover of its fourth annual Design Awards issue in May 1995. Hodgins was one of the three award recipients that year. Mr. and Mrs. Bernon admired Hodgins's work that they had seen at friends' houses and in the design magazines they read. They "had set their sights on him prior to breaking ground" for their large shingle-style house. Hodgins in turn "didn't begin the job until he learned as much as he could about Mr. and Mrs. Bernon and their visions for the house."

For his entire career, Hodgins's primary goal has been to know and understand his clients. His keen observations and astute interpretations of them, along with their hard-earned input, enables him to decorate according to "who they are, what they are and how they want to live." Hodgins "is one hundred percent for his clients" and "wants the best for them."

All of Hodgins's commissions evolve as a work in progress. Initially, he meets with clients at his office where he does not "present people with total schemes," but rather conducts his own version of a Rorschach test, asking them "to pick and choose from up to one hundred and fifty samples and discuss them in terms of texture, pattern, and color. Hodgins gets to know his clients this way, since, he says, as long as it isn't attached to their sofa or chair or [curtains], clients can express themselves freely. It's not threatening [to them]."

When Hodgins decorates for a married couple, he "insists that both husband and wife participate in the decision making and that they spend at least a day with him reviewing concepts and prospective purchases."

Rohatyn master bedroom, Paris

Hodgins's commission for the Bernons was his first in Nantucket. Initially, he found himself thinking in terms of a beach house. But after getting to know his clients, he realized that what they wanted was a summerhouse—casual in certain respects, but definitely more formal than a simple beach place.

The *Traditional Home* cover illustrated an L-shaped seating area in the Bernons' living room, a space that reflected Hodgins's well-though-out approach to his clients' preference for a "minimalist, but not stark" design. He specified painted finishes on the furniture and walls to warm the interiors. Hodgins also asked Robert Jackson to decoratively paint all of the floors in the house. His clients did not want any large rugs or carpet. Hodgins arranged the seating area with several key pieces of furniture. He anchored the grouping with a custom-made coffee table painted by Fred Browne, the fine decorative painter, adapting its design from an early nineteenth-century regency-style bench. Browne marbleized the tabletop in a grayish-white patina

and decorated its soft yellow apron in a repetitive pattern of beaded swags, which he captured in three dimensions, and corner medallions, all in pale gray.

The pièce de résistance of the seating area was a regency chair with gilded griffin carvings that Hodgins found in England. He placed the classic and stylish chair "in this pared-down setting" because "it would stand out like a jewel." The hand-painted decorative finish by Yorke Kennedy, the well-known artist frequently patronized by Hodgins, harmonized the piece within the light-filled, windowed setting.

Although Hodgins's projects during the 1990s were concentrated in New England, New York, and Florida, he also decorated houses in Nevis, Riyadh, and Paris. These three notable commissions—which spanned the period from 1994 to 1997—were all for longstanding clients.

Prince Bandar bin Khalid Al-Faisal and his wife Princess Nouf Abdullah, who commissioned Hodgins to decorate their two-bedroom duplex condominium in Beacon Hill when they attended college in Boston during the early 1990s, hired him in 1994 to decorate their home in Riyadh. The assignment lasted several years and involved two projects, one of which never materialized. Originally, the prince and princess were building a large palace for themselves and their young son. However, after extensive plans for the new home were completed, with Hodgins's participation, Prince Bandar and Princess Nouf abandoned the project. Instead, they chose to convert a wing of the palace belonging to Prince Bandar's father and make it into a "full house" for their new home.

Hodgins's design scheme for the to-be-built palace was grand. His clients selected expensive and elaborate materials, including velvets, brocades, and copiously welted upholstery—all in jewel tones. However, with the prince and princess's change of plans, they opted for a spare and simple look, one more reminiscent of their Boston apartment. The toned-down palette was also appropriate to the hot climate of Saudi Arabia. Hodgins decorated the new quarters in his characteristically elegant and restrained style. He specified pale colors and incorporated antiques and upholstered pieces from Delta/Urban LLC of New York, a favorite source of Hodgins's, where he takes his clients to show them and have them sit on muslin upholstered models of chairs and sofas, ensuring that the furniture they order from there is fitted to their individual comfort. Hodgins also shipped a large container filled with furniture to Saudi Arabia. There he used upholstery workrooms in Riyadh and Jeddah, thereby tempering the cost of the job. Even when his clients are royalty, Hodgins is always careful how he spends their money.

In 1995, Hodgins decorated a two-bedroom West Indian colonial-style villa for Julian and Eunice Cohen at the Four Seasons Resort Nevis. He furnished the biscuit-colored stucco villa in keeping with the casual and relaxed feeling of the lush Caribbean island, outfitting its great room with Bielecky Brothers furniture. Hodgins upholstered the handcrafted pale, pole rattan pieces in soft "Blue Denim" twill cushions accented with pillows in soft, fresh green solid chintz and "Mono Blue Roses"—"extravagant bouquets of roses in multi shades of blue on an off-white linen ground," hand-printed by Bennison Fabrics. The gentle and luxuriant colors emanated from the backdrop of white walls and the natural-hued wooden cathedral ceilings were amplified by the blue-and-white grid-patterned rag rugs anchoring the tiled floor of the great room.

When Felix Rohatyn was nominated to serve as the U.S. Ambassador to France, he and Mrs. Rohatyn quickly commissioned Hodgins to redecorate the private quarters in the grand and "massive" neoclassical-style mansion in Paris that would serve as their ambassadorial residence. Because the State Department strictly prohibits an ambassador's spouse

from redecorating the new home ahead of the confirmation, Hodgins was on hold until, after Mr. Rohatyn's confirmation, he "flew to Paris on Mr. and Mrs. Rohatyn's behalf to get a feeling for the rooms and their light." He also conferred with Mark Hampton, who had decorated the private quarters for Mr. Rohatyn's predecessor, Pamela Harriman. Hampton, who was "utterly gracious about facilitating the transition, [sent Hodgins] the floor plans and swatches of the paint, carpeting and [curtains]."

Mr. and Mrs. Rohatyn, who carefully shield their private lives, asked Hodgins to create "a comfortable private home within a large public residence." Mrs. Rohatyn wanted the "private floor to be cozy and beckoning"—infused "with a feeling of American informality." She wanted something that, in her words, would be "conducive to quiet suppers, intimate teas, family visits and weekends of reading."

Mrs. Rohatyn met Hodgins at his office in Boston and together they worked to choose "a color scheme that was

Rohatyn master bedroom, Paris

warmer and more European than the one at their New York home." Together they arrived at a style that Hodgins described as "an American [variation] on English country, with printed materials used discreetly and antiques mixed with comfortably streamlined sofas and chairs." Hodgins and Lucien Allaire, his design assistant, returned to Paris, where they toured the State Department warehouse on the outskirts of the city with Vivien Woofter, the director of Interiors and Furnishings at the U.S. Department of State. Although the repository was filled with "a cache of desks, commodes, armoires and tables," they only requisitioned a few pieces, including a signed eighteenth-century chair by Georges Jacob, the esteemed French cabinetmaker.

The project was challenging. Hodgins used a good deal of the furniture that had been in the private quarters, but he also needed to fill the void created by the removal of furniture that was reclaimed by Ambassador Harriman's family. Delta/Urban and Star Upholstery in the Boston area made the new pieces. Finelines, another Boston-area workshop patronized by Hodgins, made the curtains. Finelines even provided a curtain maker to fly to Paris to measure and later to install the finished work.

Robert Mercier, who worked as a decorator for the U.S. Embassy and other official American residences in Paris, was very helpful to Hodgins and Allaire. Mercier arranged for workshops in Paris to reupholster many pieces of furniture and to have the living room, and several other rooms in the private quarters, painted and glazed by very good decorative painters. In forty years Hodgins had gone from delivering groceries from the basement of the American Embassy to decorating the quarters of the American ambassador there.

As he and Mrs. Rohatyn had planned, Hodgins toned down the formality of the living room. He directed the painters to glaze the boiserie in soft beige strié. He also "resisted the impulse to overstuff" the large salon, preferring to "flatter the shapely windows and lovely garden views." His uncluttered plan entailed two seating areas he underscored with a custom-made wool rug patterned in a large-scale damask design in yellow and cream. The principal arrangement, which sat on axis to the fireplace on the opposite side of the room, was generous and restful. Hodgins specified gauffrage chenille in soft butter-saffron yellow for the oversized sofa, emphasizing the restful colors of the floral chintz he used on accent pillows and the accompanying pair of painted bergères. He also created the ideal backdrop for Mr. and Mrs. Rohatyn's collection of old master and Impressionist paintings that they brought with them from New York.

The olive-green silk damask covering the fireside ottoman contributed another dimension of color to the living room. It also complemented the chenille and floral chintz upholstery that Hodgins repeated on the sofa and chairs grouped by the fireplace. The seating area, cozy and intimate, was conducive to relaxed gatherings in the imposing reception room.

Ambassador and Mrs. Rohatyn's private quarters included a main dining room and a small dining room. Hodgins freshened up the small dining room, used for breakfast meetings and small luncheons. A good deal of state business ended up being conducted in this room because conversation was "encouraged by the intimacy of the space." Hodgins retained the brown flannel walls and French chairs that were upholstered in deep apricot flannel, but added decorative-painted tole candlelit wall sconces. He also added silk taffeta swags to the existing curtains and a large mirror over the Louis XVI–style console desserte.

The main dining room was a central space within the private quarters and therefore did not have natural light. Although Hodgins worked with Hampton's design scheme, he enhanced the lighting in the room with candles and lamps. The resulting soft light illuminated the soft yellow glaze of the paneled walls and the aged patina of the folding screen whose panels were covered in nineteenth-century Zuber wallpaper depicting an American scene.

In the Rohatyns' master bedroom Hodgins humanized the proportions of the space with "tactile [materials] and soft colors," which transformed the room into an airy suite. He used Bennison floral material hand-printed with "generous, big and full bouquets of roses in soft-to-brilliant shades of corals, pinks and crimson with stems, leaves and vines in soothing celadon green." He also used the material for the English-style curtains, which "gave the bedroom atmosphere."

Hodgins completed the commission for Mr. and Mrs. Rohatyn in the "high-speed course" of ten weeks from "start to finish." Fortunately, the installation went "flawlessly— no mistakes." Mercier had all the furniture unpacked and placed in the rooms by the time Hodgins and his team arrived at the residence, including a pair of oversized mirrors that were "shipped from Boston to Miami to France and arrived unbroken." By any standard, it was a triumph for him. The success of the assignment inspired Elizabeth Rohatyn to give a party for "the artisans and the installers. [They] were gratified and a little surprised when their hostess made a thank-you speech in fluent French."

William Hodgins continued to be recognized and acknowledged as one of the foremost interior decorators in America well into the new millennium. In 2001, ASID named Hodgins the "Designer of Distinction," one of its most prestigious awards. The award "recognizes an ASID professional interior designer who has made outstanding contributions toward achieving design excellence. The award is based on the winner's professional achievements, as exemplified by his or her work, which must demonstrate creative and innovative concepts that have advanced the profession of interior design." The New England Design Hall of Fame honored Hodgins in 2007—its inaugural year. The award, which was created jointly by the Boston Design Center and *New England Home* magazine, honored his contributions to his field and the community. The Hall of Fame, which is located in the courtyard fronting the Design Center, commemorates each inductee with a newly planted birch tree, accompanied by a plaque and the designer's signature in mortar. An honorary doctorate followed when the Boston Architectural College recognized Hodgins with a Doctor of Interior Design, Honoris Causa, at its 120th commencement exercises in 2009.

Hodgins was honored by *House Beautiful* in 2011 and *Elle Décor* in 2011 and 2012. *House Beautiful*, in its April 2011 issue, included "a special pull-out poster highlighting the genealogy of American interior designers." The placard bearing Hodgins's name branches out from the Parish-Hadley division of *House Beautiful's* "Family Tree" of "trail-blazing" interior designers "who have wowed us with their style." *Elle Décor*, in its June 2011 and 2012 issues, listed William Hodgins as one of America's "Grand Masters of Design who have defined American style."

As of this writing, Bill Hodgins is in his fifth decade of decorating under the designation of his own firm. The majority of his commissions have been carried out for repeat and loyal clients, many whom he has worked for since the day he started on his own. He has completed as many as a dozen projects for one couple and even a few more than that for members of the same family. Hodgins is also sought out by new clients, many who grew up knowing about his work, were drawn to it in person, or read about it in magazine and newspaper articles. Fortunately for Hodgins's clients, he has always cared about his work and is totally absorbed by it. And for Hodgins himself, his career as one of the finest decorators in America has been and continues to be a source of achievement, enjoyment, and fulfillment.

The interiors included here, ranging from classical tradition to modern, give a broad picture of the breadth and inimitable accomplishments of Hodgins's ongoing career. The sequence is chronological.

William Hodgins birch tree

MR. AND MRS. FELIX ROHATYN

New York, New York, 1979

Felix and Elizabeth Rohatyn asked Hodgins for a "relaxed feel" in their first commission with him—a Georgian-style duplex apartment on Park Avenue in New York. Although Hodgins decorated the apartment with a collection of heirlooms, antiques, and nineteenth-century Impressionist paintings, he created an "informal" and "spontaneous" setting conducive to his clients' casual way of living.

ENTRANCE HALL

Herringbone parquet floor that Robert Jackson stained in four shades of brown underscored a collection of fine antiques, including a mirror-surmounted Italian cabinet, an eighteenth-century English tall clock, and a steel-and-glass lantern. The archway opposite the staircase opens to the apartment's elevator vestibule.

**LIVING ROOM
TOWARD FIREPLACE**

A floral needlepoint carpet based on a nineteenth-century Bessarabian model infused pale shades of rose and green into the living room while serving as the foundation for an eclectic mélange of antiques. An eighteenth-century Venetian mirror, a Chinese panel coffee table, and a mid-eighteenth-century fauteuil covered in antique needlepoint reflected Hodgins's skillful blend of styles. The entranceway at the rear of the living room frames a view into the dining room/library.

LIVING ROOM CLOSEUP

The floral brown chintz covering the living room split-back upholstered chair, ottoman, and pillows relaxed the interior and gave it an informal feeling more akin to a country house than a Park Avenue apartment. The Impressionist oil painting hanging above the English rosewood and gilt cabinet harmonized flawlessly with the casualness of the room.

LIVING ROOM TOWARD WINDOW

Pale cream-and-white strié walls and silk taffeta curtains in sunny yellow brightened the living room and compensated for its shortage of natural light. The oval-backed Italian chair, with its apple-green patterned and textured silk upholstery, also contributed color to the interior.

DINING ROOM/LIBRARY

Hodgins incorporated built-in bookcases in the dining room because his clients are avid readers and their apartment did not have a library. He anchored the intimate interior with a nineteenth-century French country dining table and oval-backed Louis XVI chairs that were covered in tobacco-brown leather. The soft-beige French cotton check lining the backs of the dining chairs and the geometric-patterned carpet symbolized Hodgins's attention to "tone" and "texture."

MASTER BEDROOM

Mr. and Mrs. Rohatyn's master bedroom was striking with its overall application of Rose Cumming cabbage rose English chintz. The classic material covering the bedroom walls, upholstered pieces, and bed coverings filled the interior in fresh shades of rose red, pink, and green. The treasures in the bedroom included a nineteenth-century japanned cabinet, a French terra-cotta bust, and an English print after Canaletto. *Architectural Digest* featured Mr. and Mrs. Rohatyn's master bedroom on the cover of the May 1983 issue. The cover was "a nice surprise" for Mr. and Mrs. Rohatyn.

MR. AND MRS. ROBERT MONKS

Cape Elizabeth, Maine, 1981

Robert and Millicent Monks hired Hodgins to decorate and design, in collaboration with New York architect Jack P. Coble, a second-floor addition for a seaside "guest-house-turned-home" in Cape Elizabeth, Maine. The contemporary building stood on 200 acres of "coastal forest and farmland" that had been in Mrs. Monk's family for several generations. The present commission was Hodgins's third assignment for Mr. and Mrs. Monks. He had decorated their principal homes in Boston and Washington, D.C., which Mrs. Monks proclaimed were also "Masterpieces!"

ENTRANCE HALL

A console table supported by a pair of late-nineteenth-century marble brackets carved in the likeness of calves harmonized with a bronze torso, contemporary art, and a lustrous green ceramic rain drum. The eclectic arrangement foreshadowed a house filled with one-of-a-kind, out-of-the-ordinary art, furniture, and accessories, many of which were family heirlooms that came from the original old main house on the property.

LIVING ROOM REFLECTION

Hodgins broadened the parameters of the open, tall-ceilinged living room and its compelling view of "casually landscaped" land that rolled from a rear deck wrapping the house down to the Atlantic Ocean. He incorporated an expansive mirrored panel into a primary wall of the great room, empowering the natural light that filtered through a wide span of full-length windows overlooking the grassy lawn.

The mirrored wall also became the backdrop for the principal seating area. An amply scaled sofa covered in warm beige Haitian cotton and accented with pale orange and moss-green pillows melded with a seventeenth-century linen and lacquer Chinese coffee table and substantial French bergères upholstered in taupe suede. The handpainted Portuguese end table, octagonal Persian side table inlaid with mother-of-pearl, and dignified family portraits hanging in the room also augmented the uplifting low-key décor that Mr. and Mrs. Monks, who are year-round residents, "could enjoy for twelve months of the year."

DINING ROOM

The "open and inviting" floor plan of the house also organized the dining room overlooking the rear deck and Maine seacoast. The dining table, which was handsomely set with botanical-decorated porcelain and modern crystal and silver, and accessorized with an antique Chinese porcelain tomato and a pair of dolphin-based hurricane candlesticks, validated that "the rooms [in the house] were intended for entertaining."

LIVING ROOM TOWARD FIREPLACE

Hodgins created multiple seating areas in the living room. He placed an L-shaped armless sofa into a corner of the room that was arranged with tall built-in bookcases and adjoined with the fireplace wall. The oversized chair angled by the fireplace proffered an idyllic place to relax on cold New England nights or during interludes of keyboard melodies.

MR. AND MRS. E. TAYLOR CHEWNING JR.

Washington, D.C., 1981

Taylor and Mary Chewning, on the heels of Hodgins's decoration of their house in Newport, commissioned him to work on their house in Washington, D.C., a design that was more contemporary than their previous residence. The end result of the project was "a home of intriguing dualities: part urban, part suburban; part contemporary, part traditional."

The architectural plan of the house allowed Hodgins to treat the living room and dining room, which both had exposed wood-beamed ceiling and gabled rooflines, as separate pavilions. He gave each room a different color scheme and "a character of its own," taking his cues from Mr. and Mrs. Chewning's diverse collection of eighteenth- and nineteenth-century art and antiques.

LIVING ROOM TOWARD SCREEN

Hodgins decorated the living room in deference to Mr. and Mrs. Chewning's art rather than the architecture of the house. He painted the walls a light hue and emphasized his clients' large early nineteenth-century Chinese painted screen. The rare screen, which Hodgins placed across the entire width of the principal wall, consisted of eight panels of canvas that were meticulously painted to resemble a coromandel screen. Hodgins counterbalanced the exotic backdrop of the living room with a sofa covered in ecru silk, a pair of oversized armchairs luxuriously upholstered in dark-blue silk velvet, and a Karl Springer goatskin parchment coffee table. The salmon-pink leather on the pair of Louis XVI–style oval-back bergères contributed additional texture and distinction to the interior.

LIVING ROOM TOWARD CHEST

The European chinoiserie japanned chest standing at the far end of the living room reinforced the Oriental theme in the interior. Its highly lacquered patina, resonating throughout the room, was complemented by the texture and jewel-toned colors of the silk pillows on the sofa and chairs. The end table lamps—whose bases were eighteenth-century painted and gilded urns—and the antique Japanese blue-and-white vase on the coffee table exemplified the singular accessories in the living room.

DINING ROOM

The dining room was private and intimate. Hodgins decorated it traditionally to accommodate a collection of family heirlooms. He glazed and lacquered the walls in an unusual shade of brandy and lined them with several generations of family portraits, enlivening the likenesses against the distinctive hue.

The furnishings were appropriate to the setting: an eighteenth-century Georgian sideboard, which displayed a large Delft bowl given to Chewning ancestors by George Washington, a luminous regency crystal chandelier, and a long oval-shaped dining table, which converted into two tables, and chairs that Hodgins designed to "synchronize with the period pieces." His "modern and lighthearted approach" in the dining room and living room referenced history while lightening the "weight" of it.

MR. AND MRS. JULIAN COHEN

Boston, Massachusetts, 1981

Hodgins's commission for Julian and Eunice Cohen in 1981 followed several projects that he had completed for them: a duplex apartment in Back Bay, a house in Maine, and an apartment in Palm Beach. The present project, a penthouse apartment in a new building, also in Back Bay, was the most "compact place" he had decorated for Mr. and Mrs. Cohen. Fortunately, the pied-à-terre's intimate scale disseminated amidst Hodgins's and his clients' special taste, his skillful design of the bare space, and the enduring panoramic views of "traditional Boston features," including the Charles River, the Public Garden, and the "newly germinated skyscrapers" in the city's financial district.

LIVING ROOM TOWARD SKYLINE

Hodgins unified the living room's principal seating area with neutral shades and subtle textures. He upholstered the sofa in checkerboard-patterned woven silk and arranged a mixture of antique French chairs around a Karl Springer goatskin coffee table. The chairs, which were of the Louis XV and Louis XVI periods, were noteworthy. Their intricately carved and detailed framework and finely woven and embroidered silk upholstery enhanced the understated elegance of the setting.

LIVING ROOM CORNER

A glimpse of the penthouse's wraparound dove-gray limestone terrace offset an intimate seating area placed in a corner of the living room. The diminutive curved channel-back sofa with its off-white textured silk upholstery, delicately embroidered silk pillow, and Karl Springer table in Lucite evoked Hodgins's mastery of noncolors. The mixture of accessories on the coffee table included Chinese lacquered boxes; a square, decorated creamware plate; and a cachepot by Roy Hamilton, the renowned ceramicist whose work is favored by Hodgins and the late Albert Hadley and the late Sister Parish.

DINING ROOM CLOSEUP

An antique French highback chair upholstered in a pale floral print contributed to the handsomely appointed dining table. The tableware, linens, and centerpiece of pink agapanthus and lilies complemented the colors of the chair's delicately patterned material.

DINING ROOM

Hodgins filled the dining room with restrained color and superlative decorative finishes. Jay Friedline, the well-known decorative artist, marbleized and gilded the dining table and Robert Jackson painted the room's screen.

The mixture of chairs was also unique to the dining room—but not for Hodgins, who often combines furniture from different periods, especially chairs, which are an affinity of his. Here, he harmonized a pair each of antique French highback chairs and regency-style open-back chairs, enhancing the distinctive and stylish elegance of the room.

MASTER BEDROOM CLOSEUP

A linen press that Yorke Kennedy painted in a botanical theme enhanced the bedroom's charm. The lyre chair, with its classic painted and giltwood frame, and seat luxuriously upholstered in apple-green silk velvet gauffrage, contributed singularity to the bedroom.

MASTER BEDROOM

Hodgins also decorated Mr. and Mrs. Cohen's master bedroom against the backdrop of the Boston skyline. He specified a "minor blast of blue" for the bedroom, enhancing the soft color through the use of subtle patterns, including the room's curtains, paper-backed chintz applied to the walls, and carpet, all of which were off-white with traces of blue.

Essential to the bedroom's décor were its bed dressings. The floral-patterned canopy, headboard upholstery, pillows, and bedskirt were all handpainted in delicate shades of violet, blue, green, and yellow.

MR. AND MRS. JULIAN COHEN

Palm Beach, Florida, 1983

In 1982, Julian and Eunice Cohen purchased a 36-room Palm Beach regency-style house with three acres of grounds stretching from the Atlantic Ocean to Lake Worth. The house was designed by John L. Volk, the prominent Palm Beach architect, built in 1973 by Robert W. Gottfried, the well-respected Palm Beach builder, and renovated for the Cohens by James Woolems, principal of Woolems, Inc., the preeminent Florida general contracting firm. The commission was Hodgins's third project in Palm Beach for Mr. and Mrs. Cohen. It was also one of the most significant assignments of his career.

LIVING ROOM SITTING AREAS

Hodgins arranged an intimate sitting area on the far side of the living room, near the fireplace, which was surmounted by a painted and gilded nineteenth-century Italian window turned into a mirror. Here, a curved sofa, Louis XVI fauteuil, and tufted highback slipper chair were upholstered, respectively, in the damask, silk, and textured materials used throughout the living room. The coffee table was made by Karl Springer. However, Hodgins chose a parsons-style model, finished it in ivory lacquer, and detailed it with brass inlay. The gilded bronze and glass low spiral table and rare eighteenth-century Louis XV fauteuil upholstered in Italian silk damask exemplified Hodgins's credo that "the character of [a room] comes from things around the upholstered pieces."

The definitive suite of curtains dressing the windows rivaled haute couture. Hodgins specified a reversed French pleat heading for the Scalamandré textured silk overcurtains that were gathered onto gilded rings and hung from a fluted pole with finials. The curtains fronted very elaborate, softly swagged cloud shades composed of ivory silk taffeta. The antique Baccarat crystal chandelier, which was not electrified, and pair of diminutive carved Italian Rococo giltwood mirrors enhanced the setting.

LIVING ROOM

Hodgins created a living room for Mr. and Mrs. Cohen that was even more exceptional than the breathtaking views it framed of the ocean through three consecutive, expansive floor-to-ceiling windows. He started with Mrs. Cohen's inherently fine editing and favored color palette, decorating the elliptically shaped salon in the palest shades of blue, cream, and beige.

Hodgins "downplayed" the formality of the living room, underscoring it with a specially designed and colored wool Dhurrie carpet inspired by fragments of nineteenth-century French Savonnerie carpets. The present carpet, with its ivory ground, was decorated in a neoclassical garden pattern of random sprays of flowers in blues, greens, and gold on a beige trellis field. The restrained design was completed by a center medallion, bordered with a blue, beige, and green flowering vine motif.

The living room was composed of three seating areas radiating around a large skirted round table situated off-center to enhance flow in the room. One of the principal arrangements, which fronted the center window overlooking the ocean, was anchored by a large rolled-arm sofa upholstered in Scalamandré ivory trellis-patterned cotton damask. An oversized armchair covered in ivory damask and a Louis XVI fauteuil upholstered in sky-blue woven silk offset the sofa and balanced the Chinese-style coffee table that was inlaid with ivory, finished in ivory lacquer, and detailed in gold leaf.

Hodgins placed a second seating area along the south wall of the living room where he specified a rolled-arm sofa identically designed to its counterpart and upholstered in Scalamandré ivory textured material. A balanced pair of split-back upholstered chairs—one of Hodgins's favorite models from Delta/Urban—covered in ivory damask, a Louis XVI fauteuil, and a lacquered goatskin waterfall coffee table from Karl Springer contributed subtle variations between the two seating arrangements.

LOGGIA

Volk's plan for the formal level of the house included a loggia, a casual and inviting sitting area that flowed off the living room and opened onto an expansive covered veranda overlooking the swimming pool and Intracoastal waterway.

Hodgins struck a perfect chord when decorating the loggia. He applied his palette of texture and noncolors, creating an interior that did not impose on the splendor of the living room or tranquil view of the waterway. He also designed less-elaborate cloud shades, which were appropriate to the interior and complemented the curtains in the living room.

First and foremost was the distinctive floor. Exotic black walnut parquet arranged diagonally was inlaid with eighteen-inch squares of cream-colored veined onyx that were interspersed in a windowpane pattern of four throughout the room.

Hodgins unified two seating areas with a Berber carpet hand-knotted in ivory wool. He placed a rolled-arm sofa at one end of the carpet, grouping it with a Louis XVI–style racetrack oval coffee table in walnut and stone, made by Frederick P. Victoria, and a pair of large régence-style open armchairs upholstered in pale taupe leather. Fortuny in pale white on beige covered the sofa and the accompanying pair of armchairs and ottoman.

The loggia was furnished with a Karl Springer game table, made in goatskin, highly lacquered and detailed with brass. The pairs of Louis XVI–style Cole Porter game chairs, made by Frederick P. Victoria in two designs, injected both Art Deco and chinoiserie into the interior.

DINING ROOM TOWARD SERVER

Hodgins paired an opulently detailed and gilded Louis Philippe mirror with a custom server that he designed and Yorke Kennedy painted and decorated in the classical manner. The arrangement added to the grandeur of the dining room.

DINING ROOM

Hodgins maintained the soft-blue and off-white color scheme in the dining room. He furnished it with an oval-shaped double-pedestal table painted by Jay Friedline in shades of pale stone, encircled with a band of faux lapis. The table, which sat on a wool and silk medallion-patterned carpet, was accompanied by oval-back dining chairs, upholstered alternately in pale yellow leather and yellow-and-white ribbon-patterned damask. Silk taffeta curtains in pale sky blue and white—composed of alternating panels of each color that were seamed together—framed the intimate breakfast bay overlooking the Intracoastal waterway.

The dining room's noteworthy pieces included an English Georgian crystal chandelier and post-Impressionist art. The Louis XVI–style console with its pierced apron, additional carved details, and marble top made by Frederick P. Victoria displayed blue-and-white Canton porcelain.

POOLSIDE LOGGIA

Volk's innovative plan created a downstairs loggia that opened to the swimming pool terrace, and several rooms, including two guest suites, the octagonal wine cellar, and underground passageway leading from the house, below South Ocean Boulevard, to the Cohens' private beach.

Hodgins gave the downstairs loggia, the most informal room in the house, a casual and relaxed feeling. He outfitted the room with Bielecky Brothers furniture, covering the cushions of the handcrafted pale, pole rattan pieces in stone-ground cotton canvas.

The canvas, printed by Leslie Tillett and D. D. Tillett, was patterned in complementary designs in blue and white—a random stripe dotted with confetti, and a peony. The Dhurrie carpet, which was geometric patterned in various shades of beige, and the lacquered Chinese low tables added contrast to the room.

MASTER BEDROOM

An elaborately carved and dressed canopy bed complemented a collection of fine French furniture, including the Louis XV desk that Yorke Kennedy painted to replicate the off-white French silk taffeta covering the bed pillows, the Louis XVI–style bench, and the Louis XV chair. The armchair and ottoman, upholstered in soft blue cotton woven texture, contributed a spray of color to the monochromatic décor.

BLACK-AND-WHITE GUEST ROOM

Mr. and Mrs. Cohen "so loved" the black-and-white guest room that Hodgins decorated for them in their first Palm Beach apartment that "they insisted it be duplicated" when they moved to the house.

The guest room was equally splendid in its second rendition. The walls were lacquered a bright shiny black, contrasting dramatically with the delicate white lace curtains and bedcoverings and the ornately carved Indian-style wooden screen with pierced detailing that Hodgins painted white. The spare embroidery of pansies patterned on the upholstered headboard, bed pillows, and gathered bed skirt also perfected the interior.

VIEW TOWARD THE FRENCH COMMODE

The Louis XV French commode, which
Yorke Kennedy decoratively painted in ivory
and bone, contributed additional color and
softness to the dramatic interior. The white
paneled wainscoting also highlighted the
depth and quality of the black glazing.

GUEST ROOM SITTING AREA

Hodgins arranged a comfortable sitting area along the wall
opposite the bed. He maintained the whiteness and subtle
texture of the room, upholstering the sofa, French wing
chair, and ottoman in cotton damask and printed cotton.

Hodgins also used soft colors in the setting, dispersing
colors with the pillows, wool throw, decoupaged lamps, and
hand-painted coffee table. The brackets flanking the landscape
oil painting displayed enameled metal plates.

MS. SOPHIE ENGELHARD

Sun Valley, Idaho, 1984

Hodgins's fourth project for Sophie Engelhard was the interior decoration of her small adobe-style house in Sun Valley, Idaho. The house, which stands on twelve acres, 9,000 feet above the valley, has three mesmerizing views. Ms. Engelhard essentially has her own canyon.

Initially, Hodgins, along with Sun Valley architect Janet Jarvis, "simplified the architecture" of the house. He removed a portion of the living room wall, creating openness within the interior.

Hodgins, taking his cue from the "ruggedness of the architecture," specified doors of hard pine that he had trimmed in textured stucco—an "essential element of the house." He also stuccoed the house's three stone fireplaces to enhance the intensity of whiteness that Ms. Engelhard loves.

LIVING ROOM

Hodgins specified warm colors in the living room, taking them from the Clarence House cotton paisley covering the recamier. He chose aubergine and moss green, using these lush colors in solid materials for the pair of oversized armchairs and chaise longue. The rag carpet, which was hand-loomed in Vermont, was composed of colors from taupe to brown.

Ms. Engelhard's living room is not only comfortable and practical, but it also embodies Hodgins's ritual of using "everything [of his client's], and filling in where need be. He wastes nothing." The recamier and lacquered Karl Springer goatskin coffee table, with its pullout backgammon board, were originally installed by Hodgins in Ms. Engelhard's Boston apartment.

DINING ROOM

The cotton paisley was also handsome on the tufted dining chairs. Its taupe ground and multicolored print complemented Ms. Engelhard's late-nineteenth-century French pedestal table with carved hound motif base and characterful antique American cupboard. The bare terra-cotta floor and tree-trunk supports enhanced the rustic setting.

SITTING ROOM

Hodgins decorated Ms. Engelhard's sitting room against a compelling view of the Boulder mountain range. He used colors of nature, upholstering the sofa in a textured material in mouse brown and accenting it with pale gold pillows. The rag rug, which replicated the carpet in the living room, infused natural colors into the interior. Additional character came from the old pine trunk and adobe fireplace.

BEDROOM SITTING AREA

Ms. Engelhard wanted her house to be cozy and comfortable. Hodgins was more than successful. The sitting area by the bedroom fireplace has become a cherished spot. The paintings hanging throughout the bedroom are portraits of Engelhard's beloved dogs.

MASTER BEDROOM

When Ms. Engelhard announced to Hodgins that she wanted an all-white bedroom, he laughed and said, "Madame, have you forgotten that you have six dogs?" Hodgins—who is a great animal lover himself—knew what would be appropriate for his client and her Golden Retrievers and Labs.

Hodgins used glazed cotton chintz, in a small leaf pattern, as the predominant material. He complemented the spare, but vibrant print with cotton material boldly striped in irregular divisions of pale red, lavender, and gold. Robert Jackson painted Engelhard's oversized fanciful nineteenth-century bed.

MR. AND MRS. ROBERT TAUBMAN

San Francisco, California, 1985

When Robert and Linda Taubman redecorated their pied-à-terre on San Francisco's Nob Hill, they called on Bill Hodgins to do the job. Mr. and Mrs. Taubman appreciated working with Hodgins on their Detroit house and looked forward with great enthusiasm to their second project with him. The third-floor apartment, which was not large, overlooked Grace Cathedral and Huntington Park.

DRAWING ROOM DESK

The nineteenth-century Viennese Biedermeier desk augmented the collection of fine furniture in the drawing room. The rounded desk was especially unusual. Its supporting columns, which were lined, had removable tops, allowing them to hold cut flowers. The giltwood English oval-back chair sitting at the desk was one of a pair placed in the drawing room.

SITTING/DINING ROOM

Hodgins created a seamless transition between the drawing room and the sitting/dining room, a room that he adapted from the original dining room. The revised plan relaxed the inherent formality of the apartment.

Muted colors, additional Biedermeier pieces, and contemporary furniture composed the sitting/dining room. The bronze and glass coffee table was underscored by an antique Samarkand carpet that was "so faded and worn," it was barely noticeable on the glossy bleached wood floor. The sofa was covered in striped linen in beige and ivory and accessorized with antique needlepoint and silver silk damask pillows.

DRAWING ROOM

Hodgins and his clients agreed on a design that was "spare," "voluptuous," and sensitive to the apartment's elaborate Beaux-arts detailing.

The tall French doors in the drawing room, which overlooked the park, were dressed in pale sea-blue silk taffeta and simplified by rattan shades. The furniture was upholstered in subtly textured materials: creamy silk ottoman cloth for the sofa and creamy white silk damask on the eighteenth-century English oval-back chair.

Mr. and Mrs. Taubman enjoyed shopping for the apartment with Hodgins. Their visit to London resulted in several extraordinary acquisitions, including the open-arm Biedermeier chair with ebonized detailing and early nineteenth-century Russian burled-elm chair with ormolu mounts. The double doorway in the background framed a view of the adjacent sitting/dining room.

MASTER BEDROOM

Mr. and Mrs. Taubman's "romantic" master bedroom, with its canopy bed sumptuously draped in Scottish white cotton lace, was on the cover of the August 1988 issue of *Architectural Digest*. The diaphanous quality of the material was intensified by the soft blue silk sunburst of the canopy and the marbleized gray-green-and-white floor painted by Robert Jackson.

MASTER BEDROOM FIREPLACE

A floral-bouquet-and-ribbon-patterned chintz adorned the armchair and ottoman arranged in a corner of the bedroom, alongside the fireplace. The early eighteenth-century Louis XVI gilded oval mirror reflected the bedroom's natural light and offset a collection of miniature topiary trees from Eric Cogswell, the Northern California designer.

MR. AND MRS. FELIX ROHATYN

New York, New York, 1986

When Felix and Elizabeth Rohatyn commissioned Hodgins to decorate their New York apartment, he first restored the full-floor prewar residence to its original integrity. Hodgins's "biggest job was making it look as though it belonged again, to create a design that was appropriate both for the 1916 building and [his clients]." He reorganized the floor plan, beginning at the elevator foyer, which he combined with the front hall, allowing "an immediate view into the living room and to the cityscape outside."

Hodgins and his staff designed cornice moldings, baseboards, and chair railings, reinterpreting the original architectural elements that had been "stripped" by the apartment's previous owners. He also separated the rooms with specially made French doors, designing them with glass panes on top and paneled divisions below, instilling a source of light as well as a sense of privacy throughout the apartment.

LIVING ROOM SITTING AREA

Hodgins arranged a sitting area in the living room to create intimacy. He angled a curved tufted-back sofa across a corner of the room, alongside an antique Chinese carpet and against the backdrop of an upholstered three-panel folding screen. Scalamandré antique-white damask covered the sofa and the tufted and fringed "Hadley" chair (named for Albert Hadley) was upholstered in old rose English chintz, maintaining the consistency of design in the room. The gray painted Louis XVI cane-back armchair, with its Scalamandré raspberry textured damask seat cushion, custom cord trim, and copious tassels, and the parsons-style coffee table—in the Anglo-Chinese style, finished in soft pewter by Yorke Kennedy—completed the comfortable arrangement.

LIVING ROOM AT FIREPLACE

Hodgins organized the living room into two seating areas, creating the division with an antique Russian desk that he centered in the room. The principal sofa, which fronted the desk and aligned with the fireplace, balanced a pair of split-back chairs upholstered in Scalamandré antique-white damask. Old rose English chintz, printed in hues of raspberry and green on off-white ground, covered the button-tufted ottoman sitting before the fireplace and infused restrained shades of color into the setting. The pivotal early eighteenth-century Venetian mirror and antique French mantel enhanced the traditional nuances in the room.

DINING ROOM

Classically paneled walls glazed pale cream created an elegant backdrop in the dining room, which was arranged with French Louis XVI antiques. The late-eighteenth-century brass-mounted mahogany dining table was surrounded by oval-back chairs, finished in old-world white, and upholstered in brown leather with contrasting soft-beige French cotton check on their outside backs. The demi-lune commode was late eighteenth century, surmounted by a pair of electrified Directoire giltwood bras de lumières. Bookcases built into three corners of the dining room instilled "a pleasing informality" to the interior.

DINING ROOM CLOSEUP

Luxurious curtains of alternating striped panels of Scalamandré cream and rose silk taffeta seamed together, and an eighteenth-century French three-panel canvas screen painted with various landscapes, chinoiserie reserves, trophies, and initials enlivened and personalized the dining room. The classically paneled walls, chair railing, and cornice moldings restored the dining room to its period elegance.

LIBRARY
(ABOVE AND PREVIOUS PAGES)

Hodgins furnished the library against the backdrop of a neutral tableau. He glazed the walls in ivory strié, dressed the windows, and upholstered the sofa, tufted chair, and ottoman in ivory herringbone-patterned raw silk from Jack Lenor Larsen. Noncolors of embossed leather covered the pair of Italian régence-style open armchairs flanking the English renters' desk placed alongside the window. A large French chair, upholstered in a Clarence House chinoiserie printed cotton with vignettes of figures, water vessels and pagodas separated by an undulating leopard stripe on a cream ground, highlighted the interior. The French doors re-created a "sensible progression" between the library and living room.

LIBRARY CLOSEUP

Floor-to-ceiling bookcases arranged with small traditional lamps on several shelves contributed warmth and soft light to the library, reflecting lustrously from the seasoned patina of the antiques and coffee table glazed in creamy beige French lacquer. The loop and flat weave geometric-patterned carpet in beige and cream heightened the subtleties in the comfortable room.

MASTER BEDROOM

Hodgins placed a mid-eighteenth-century George III mahogany writing table and nineteenth-century Austrian carved side chair against the white paneled wainscoting, underscoring a collection of Italian architectural prints. The classic English chintz enlivened all facets of the interior.

MASTER BEDROOM REFLECTION

Mr. and Mrs. Rohatyn asked Hodgins to replicate the master bedroom from the Park Avenue apartment in their new home, reusing the furniture upholstered in the Rose Cumming English chintz and ordering additional material for the wainscoted walls. The profusion of stemmed cabbage roses in the chintz—in fresh shades of rose red, pink, and green—complemented the roomful of traditional furniture, including the Louis XVI–style giltwood wall mirror and nineteenth-century Chippendale-style mahogany banquette placed at the foot of the bed.

PRIVATE RESIDENCE

Middleburg, Virginia, 1986

William Hodgins "reworked" a Colonial-style house that his client purchased "in the middle of the swellest horse country in America." The handsome stone house, which stood on nearly 200 acres and was built principally during the early 1900s, contained "no interior architectural detailing," allowing Hodgins "more freedom to make changes without guilt." Paul Lanoix, from Hodgins's office, "[used] a classical vocabulary" and detailed the interior with "strong architectural elements," providing an effective backdrop for the relaxed and understated luxury created by Hodgins and the innately fine editing of his client.

Hodgins's client values the "level of detail, quality and precision" in his work and the superlative craftsmanship of the people he hires. She asked Robert Sinclair (accompanied by his wife) and his son Bobby Sinclair, who painted her Back Bay apartment, to relocate from the Boston area to Middleburg to paint her house, along with an experienced local crew they supervised. She housed the Sinclairs in the caretaker's house on her property during the three months it took to complete the assignment. When the house was finished, Hodgins encouraged his client to host a party for the contractors who worked on the renovation "over the course of so many months" and their wives "to put the house in use." The get-together gave the contractors the opportunity to show the result of their dedicated and "extraordinary" work—of which they were very proud—to their wives. It meant a lot to Hodgins's client "to let them share their creation with their loved ones."

ENTRANCE HALL

A Scottish Adamesque mantel Hodgins located at Danny Alessandro in New York dignified the entrance hall against the backdrop of walls Robert Jackson painted en grisaille to resemble dressed stone. The early eighteenth-century French régence wing chair, with its original gauffrage leather, and English rosewood pedestal stand complemented the handsome arrangement.

LIVING ROOM CLOSEUP

Robert Jackson's artistic ability enhanced the living room. He softly marbleized the walls and concealed the television and stereo equipment behind a panel he painted with classical details and books and objects favored by the client. The Gainsborough chair fronting Jackson's trompe l'oeil was upholstered in pale beige woven silk.

LIVING ROOM (OPPOSITE AND FOLLOWING PAGES)

Hodgins arranged the living room with oversized furnishings. He upholstered the sofas and chairs in off-white rough-textured silk and curtained the windows with charcoal-and-beige striped silk taffeta, which "swelled out and crumpled onto the [original wide plank pine] floor." The incorporation of exemplary antiques in the room, including the gilded regency overmantel mirror, pair of large nineteenth-century régence-style open armchairs, and nest of three Edwardian black lacquer tables, were tempered by the "edited color palette."

DINING ROOM

Pale shades of sunny yellow, and accents of cream and charcoal, created a "soft glow" in the "glamorously pared-down" dining room. The Sinclairs glazed the walls in strié and Robert Jackson embellished the chair rail frieze with dentils and rosettes. The English mahogany dining table and George III wheel-back-style chairs were underscored by a wool sisal carpet bound in canvas.

OUTBACK ROOM

Hodgins and Lanoix conceived a "separate wing of the house for casual living." The "Italian-monastic feeling of the paneled room gave the client a slightly whimsical retreat from the more classical restraint in the other part of the house." The addition's "grand and rustically simple details" included a pale dove-gray English Minster stone floor, large floor-to-ceiling shutters, and a plank ceiling. Robert Jackson's "slight wash of uneven color" added charm and patina to the new room, which Hodgins arranged with overscaled furniture upholstered in beige textured material, floral cotton chintz, and mulberry linen.

OUTBACK ROOM BY FIREPLACE

Hodgins arranged a dining area alongside the fireplace and a generously windowed corner of the room. He surrounded the nineteenth-century English mahogany pedestal dining table with Queen Anne–style chairs that were painted, gilded, and upholstered in Brunschwig & Fils mulberry linen. The outback room—with its fireplace and French doors—was welcoming throughout the year.

MR. AND MRS. CALVIN GOULD

Palm Beach, Florida, 1987

Roz Gould says she "had the best time" working with Hodgins on two projects at the same time. He also decorated her Boston condominium in 1987. Everything Hodgins showed her, she liked, which made it difficult for her to decide what to choose. Twenty-five years later, Mrs. Gould still revels in the work Hodgins did for her and her late husband.

LIVING ROOM/DINING AREA

Hodgins planned the living room as a grand salon, underscoring it with a Guatemalan natural cotton and sisal carpet. He placed a comfortable sitting area on each side of the spacious interior and equalized the dining table between the two groupings. The round table, with its imposing classical base—a carved and gilded Swedish urn swagged with garlands—was exquisitely painted by Robert Jackson in the palest shades of ivory beige and white with a softly marbleized top. The Louis XVI–style oval-back dining chairs were well suited to the arrangement.

ENTRANCE HALL

Mrs. Gould's apartment in Palm Beach is a cocoon of luxuriant ivory. Robert Jackson quoined the walls in the entrance hall, creating faux stone blocks of soft white with pale putty grouting. He also painted the floor in faux marbre, shading its checkerboard pattern in gentle hues of bone and ivory. Jackson's masterful work complemented the Italian Baroque pedestal and its wooden base. The marble-topped base, which was elaborately carved in the round and painted and gilded to look like bronze, depicted the likeness of recurring lions' heads supported by strapping legs with hefty paws.

LIVING ROOM SITTING AREA

Hodgins's symmetrical plan for the living room was enhanced by subtle variations in the furniture and accessories he chose for each sitting area. Identical models, including the sofa, coffee table, and oval mirror, were offset by chairs and end tables of varied styles and finishes. The gentle mix of pillows that Hodgins dispersed between the two groupings also complemented the balanced arrangement.

LIBRARY

Walls marbleized in soft old-world white with beige and gray veining created the ideal background in the library for a collection of Biedermeier furniture and the plush sofa, armchair, and ottoman that Hodgins upholstered in neutral-hued safari-patterned cotton. Artistic imprint also came from the parsons-style coffee table that was decoratively painted and detailed in faux ivory inlay.

MASTER BEDROOM

Hodgins maintained a background of ivory in Mrs. Gould's master bedroom and instilled it with distinctly feminine touches. He curtained the windows in white embroidered organdy and dressed the bed in a coverlet and ruffled sham of soft cream floral chintz patterned with pale gray roses and empire-green petals. The upholstered princess-shaped headboard, with its deeply sheered corners, feminized the design palette.

Hodgins outfitted the bedroom with a comfortable mixture of furniture. He specified a pair of mirrored bedside tables and painted antiques, including the Italian Louis XV–style bench placed at the foot of the bed and tasseled Sheraton armchair sitting against the bedroom wall. Robert Jackson's decorative treatment beautified the dressing table, desk, and built-in armoire.

MR. AND MRS. LEWIS LLOYD

Brookline, Massachusetts, 1987

Lewis and Linda Lloyd had already "consulted" with Hodgins about decorating their townhouse on Boston's Beacon Hill when they became "smitten" with a Gothic Revival "cottage" in Brookline, Massachusetts, and decided to make it their home. The shuttered white clapboard house, with its fanciful Gothic windows, was charming. The house was sited in a parklike setting with its front door facing a grassy lawn and narrow stream. Coincidentally, Hodgins had admired the 1826 house "long before the Lloyds bought [it]. He used to drive by [the house] and think what wonderful windows!"

Hodgins made minimal structural changes to the interior of the house. He enlarged the doorways in the living room and dining room to accommodate French doors that were scaled to "match the elegance of the rooms" and also "let light into the rooms beyond."

ENTRANCE HALL

Hodgins decorated the entrance hall with restraint. He marbleized the walls subtly, so it was "barely noticeable"—"just a whisper." The faux stone floor painted by Robert Jackson also gave the hall "old-world elegance" and complemented the spare arrangement of furniture: a painted Italian console and pair of antique painted Gothic chairs.

DINING ROOM

William Morris wallpaper hand-blocked in shades of pale gray and teal blue created a "romantic" backdrop for country French furniture in the dining room. The marbleized dining table, with its leaf border, was painted by Yorke Kennedy and the French chairs were upholstered in multicolored needlepoint trimmed in red braid. Natural light, which enhanced the interior, filtered through the pair of dining room windows that were beautifully dressed by Robert Blankenship—the Boston-area curtain maker and upholsterer—who hung lace at the top of each window and then cut it to outline and flatter the Gothic arch.

LIVING ROOM

Although the original floorplan of the house was "peculiar," and separated the living room into two rooms, Hodgins combined them, creating a large living room that was long and narrow, but causing the fireplace to be "way off-center."

Hodgins unified the living room with a single carpet, but treated each side of the room separately. On one side of the living room, he arranged a seating area to "create intimacy and focus on the fireplace," angling a sofa across a corner of the room and filling the resulting space with an eighteenth-century scenic French screen.

Soft pastel shades taken from the hollyhock-and-swag-patterned chintz of the upholstered armchair placed near the fireplace infused the interior and shaded the woven, textured, and embroidered silk materials covering the additional furniture in the grouping. Neutral colors also calmed the interior. The sofa was upholstered in an off-white jacquard and the windows were dressed in billows and ruffles of silk taffeta in pale gray—a "recessive" color that did not impose on the singularity and integrity of the Gothic design.

MASTER BEDROOM

Hodgins, who has always been passionate for "old painted finishes," anchored the master bedroom with a painted French antique bed and gave it "weight" and "contrast" with a pair of flanking night tables in dark antique and black lacquered wood. He softened the bedroom with additional painted furniture and pastel-shaded materials. Begonia-patterned chintz dressed the bed and covered the seat cushion of the barrel-back cane bergère, which was complemented by a backdrop of curtains in delicate white lace, lined with pale pink chintz.

MS. CHARLENE ENGELHARD

Concord, Massachusetts, 1987

Charlene Engelhard was a longstanding client of Hodgins's when she commissioned him to work on and decorate her house in Concord, Massachusetts. Originally, Engelhard built a big New England barn she refers to as the "Black Box" in the Boston suburb, but it was designed without windows to accommodate her art collection. In time, Engelhard found the weekend home somewhat "depressing" because of the lack of light. She then asked Hodgins to transform the large clapboard building, making it "all light" by incorporating oversized windows into its reconfigured plan and completely painting the interior white. Hodgins also designed a large carriage house, which was connected by a colonnaded passageway to the back end of the original building.

ENTRANCE HALL

Hodgins furnished the entrance hall with Engelhard's "[unusual] conglomeration of furniture." He placed a red-and-blue Tunisian tribal carpet on the tiled slate floor and amplified the bold colors and primitive overtones with an antique country pine sideboard that was painted dark green. The unique chandelier, with its swag motif, was iron and tole.

GREAT ROOM CLOSEUP

Charlene Engelhard "loves the impromptu, [and] has a talent for it. If she [likes] something, that [is] it." Her eclectic collection of carpets, country furniture, and antiques, including the farm table with a pine top and painted and distressed blue base, Italian Renaissance chairs upholstered in apple-green chenille, and Louis XV–style side chairs with old gilded and gesso finish, melded flawlessly in the distinctive and uninhibited interior.

Engelhard credits Hodgins's ability to "go beyond anything you could ever expect. He's got that great eye and finds you great stuff. [Experiencing his rooms] is like walking into a painting. It's like Christmas. You can't believe you live there."

GREAT ROOM (PREVIOUS PAGES)

Hodgins anchored the center of the great room with a principal seating area. He arranged a pair of large sofas in an L-shape opposite the fireplace, and slipcovered them in soft brown silk damask. Pillows covered in damask and French glazed floral chintz contributed sprays of soft colors to the setting.

GREAT ROOM OVERVIEW

The epicenter of the house was a large two-story great room that terminated at a tall pitched, planked, and trussed ceiling. A balustraded gallery around the perimeter of the room comprised the second floor of the generously windowed building and provided additional wall space for Engelhard's art collection and a complete view of the great room below.

GREAT ROOM AT FIREPLACE

Hodgins placed a Louis XVI provincial walnut duchesse brisée alongside the fireplace, providing a comfortable setting for reading and relaxing. The cut limestone mantel he designed, with its squared shelf and simple bracketed supports, complemented the offsetting arrangement of French provincial and Italian furniture.

DINING ROOM

The dining room, which overlooks the property through tall glazed doors, was furnished informally and eclectically. The pine farm dining table, its French provincial ladder-back and Italian open armchairs, and pine commode were in keeping with the country setting.

DINING ROOM ENTRANCE

Hodgins framed the entrance into the dining room with a pair of yellow silk portières, hanging them from a beam and reinforcing the division from the adjoining great room. The luxurious curtains, juxtaposed with rustic architectural elements and country furniture, maintained Engelhard's partiality for "a mixture of everything."

SUNROOM

Neutral colors, subtle textures, and a glazed "park bench" green tile floor composed the sunroom that Hodgins added to the house and exposed to the outdoors through three generously windowed walls. The sofa was upholstered in a beige textured material and two split-back chairs were covered in almond-green woven cotton. Country furniture, including an antique pine end table, English pine blanket chest, and green wicker armchair, maintained the rustic décor instilled throughout the house. Pillows covered in geranium-pink-and-violet strié silk taffetas and multi-lilac-colored floral chintz accented the room.

MASTER BEDROOM CLOSEUP

The eclecticism of the master bedroom ranged from a traditional eighteenth-century French corbeille, with an ornately carved frame and hunter-green strié velvet upholstery, to a collection of unassuming pine furniture. The antique pine armoire placed between the pair of arched double-hung windows was especially handsome. It was painted in a greenish-blue rubbed finish, adding to the vibrant color in the light-filled room.

MASTER BEDROOM

Hodgins infused the master bedroom with significant color. He covered the floor in a specially colored blue carpet patterned with a raspberry pindot design, dressed the bed with a multicolored floral bouquet chintz printed on a ground of teal blue, and curtained the windows with soft green textured linen. A diverse mixture of furniture, including the pine night table, whitewashed regency open armchair decorated with carved stars and soft blue striping, and painted country table with antique marbleized tiles, contributed character to the room.

MR. AND MRS. JULIAN COHEN

Palm Beach, Florida, 1988

Julian and Eunice Cohen sold their large John Volk regency-style house in 1988 and hired Hodgins to decorate and instill a "medium-size" oceanfront apartment in a modern building with the "character" and architectural detailing of their former home. Hodgins, in collaboration with his in-house team of designers and Woolems, Inc., the contracting firm that superlatively renovated the apartment, succeeded at this "very difficult" assignment. He achieved, to the justified expectations of his clients, "elegance on this [intimate] scale," giving the apartment the patina of "older, grander houses."

POWDER ROOM

Robert Jackson's "pale and musty painting of dropped white linen after the Empire style" made the powder room "feel special and different from the rest of the apartment." The trompe-l'oeil design, which was set against the "softest green," also concealed several storage closets in the room and complemented the Italian octagonal pedestal table and its handsome grouping of accessories.

LIVING ROOM AT FIREPLACE

Hodgins "edited and re-used" Mr. and Mrs. Cohen's own furniture, art, and antiques from the house. In the new living room he placed a seating area alongside an eighteenth-century Louis XV stone mantel. Elegant upholstery materials—beige satin, pale beige leather, and Italian silk damask—emanated a "divinely airy" quality and "uniformly pristine decoration in every shade of white, from ecru to ivory, from eggshell to bone" embraced by Hodgins's clients.

LIVING ROOM OVERVIEW

Hodgins arranged the living room thoughtfully, composing an interior that was natural and understated. His acknowledged restraint underplayed the rarity of the singular antiques and exemplary furniture distinguishing the room, including the pair of late eighteenth-century Louis XV fauteuils en chassis, the neoclassical patinated bronze candlesticks and their oval-shaped pedestal cabinets, and the nineteenth-century French low table with a base of gilded swans. Although the living room "flowed gently" into the dining room, Hodgins achieved a feeling of separation between the two rooms. The mirrored reflection captured the splendor and calmness of Hodgins's decorating.

DINING ROOM

A bare wooden floor of the "palest" herringbone oak parquet underscored a classic dining table that Hodgins designed with a fluted and gilded French mahogany columnar base and faux stone top. Hodgins also designed the dining room server—classically styled and softly painted by Yorke Kennedy. The Louis XVI–style oval-back open armchairs and their pale-stone leather upholstery were well suited to the arrangement.

LIBRARY

Furniture comfortably upholstered in the Clarence House chintz, "Papiers Japonais," and a wall of classically detailed built-in cabinets and bookcases instilled the library with coziness and elegance. The spare floral pattern of the vintage material also infused the interior with delicate colors that were subtly discernable among the immediate shades of ecru, ivory, and pale lustre gray. The "Korean-style" coffee table, which Hodgins designed, was wrapped in linen.

MASTER BEDROOM

A faux marbre floor exquisitely painted by Robert Jackson in a large architectural pattern and shaded in white, pale stone, and deeper stone underscored an elegantly dressed and decorated canopy bed and its flanking pair of Louis XV–style painted bedside tables and classically carved and painted Italian Louis XVI–style bench.

The bed was especially beautiful. Its callow-shaped canopy, valances, side curtains, and bedskirt were fashioned from delicate scallop-bordered white cotton lace and lined with white silk taffeta. The diaphanous tableau was also augmented by Yorke Kennedy, who painted the handsomely shaped and detailed wood headboard in a confection of frothy white lace against a neutralized ground of soft greige.

MASTER BEDROOM CORNER

Hodgins placed an upholstered armchair and ottoman against a gossamer backdrop of billowing white lace sheers and poof-headed overcurtains in woven self-striped silk. He offset the comfortable seating with a nineteenth-century painted Indian folding table, a rustic design that was resourcefully integrated with the roomful of classic French furniture. The wool throw handwoven by Leni's Inc., the renowned Boston-area textile house, complemented the ottoman and broadened the restrained shades of blue accenting the bedroom.

GUEST BEDROOM CLOSEUP

Hodgins enveloped the guest bedroom in delicate shades of off-white and sky blue. He stained the herringbone oak parquet floor faintly and covered the walls and curtained the windows in a "specially colored" cotton damask print. Large ruffled pillows—made from the damask material—accented the bed and complemented the textural quality of the white matelasse spread.

GUEST BEDROOM

Hodgins arranged the guest bedroom with a compilation of furniture from the Cohens' previous home. Several pieces, including a French-style commode, desk, and three matching benches, each of which were perfectly suited to the black-and-white guest bedroom or the blue, cream, and beige living room in the house, were repurposed flawlessly in the new suite. Whether refinished, reupholstered, or left unchanged, they all assumed a refreshed life.

On the desk, Roy Hamilton's ceramic pencil cup holds specially made white pencils—Hodgins's customary "last finishing touch" for his clients at the completion of a job.

MR. WILLIAM HODGINS

Boston, Massachusetts, 1988

In 1988, Bill Hodgins moved back to 191 Commonwealth Avenue. He always loved the building and fortunately he found a larger apartment there. Hodgins's new apartment—like the first one—was located on the second floor of the building, but because it was situated in a prime corner, the views and exposure to natural light were exceptional.

First, Hodgins fine-tuned the apartment. He moved several walls, and added tall baseboards, dentil moldings, and door casings, giving the interior architectural integrity and character. Hodgins also incorporated two arched doorways in the living room, facilitating the flow into the connecting hallway and dining room.

LIVING ROOM

In the living room, Robert Jackson replicated the dentil moldings in trompe l'oeil that Hodgins had installed throughout the apartment. Jackson deepened the profile of the moldings by one and a half inches, making them proportionate to the interior, exaggerating its height and the large bay window, which overlooked Commonwealth Avenue and was a principal source of natural light for the apartment.

Shades of white, soft gray, and natural tones "[softened] the periphery of [the] room," which was composed of textured materials, "chipped and flakey painted finishes," which Hodgins likes for their "crudeness." The room holds a mixture of contemporary upholstered and period pieces, including nineteenth-century Italian chairs and late Louis XVI and French empire models, plumbago-filled nineteenth-century English garden urns in terracotta and an overscaled stone garden statue purchased in London.

DINING ROOM

Hodgins furnished the dining room with singular pieces against the backdrop of a large window elegantly curtained in unlined celadon silk taffeta and crowned with an Italian tole pelmet. He anchored the room with a mid-nineteenth-century mahogany hall settee that he found rain soaked on a roadside in Maine, had decoratively painted by Yorke Kennedy, and reupholstered, and surmounted it with an early eighteenth-century painted and gilded Italian mirror decorated with four perching blackbirds. Hodgins purchased the mirror in London, and it complemented the pair of French empire armchairs completing the seating arrangement at the dining table.

LIVING ROOM
TOWARD FIREPLACE

Hodgins has a fondness for selecting fireplace mantels, which he says "set the character of a room." He installed several of them in the apartment, including the Louis XVI stone mantel, which was the focal point in the living room. The harmonization of chairs in the room, with their diverse origins and shapes, was flawless and created a natural and relaxed atmosphere to their placement. Hodgins likes chairs to be readily moved as needed, but "created a clear, strong structure [in the living room] with sofa, coffee table, desk, huge urns, and a garden statue" of Hercules, although its pedestal was ingeniously outfitted with wheels!

MASTER BEDROOM

Hodgins created a cozy master
bedroom with walls covered in
honey-colored natural silk and
window curtains and headboard
upholstery in the same soft-toned
material. The Georgian-style
settee at the foot of the bed,
early Queen Anne table by the
window, and late-eighteenth-
century directoire armchair
harmonized an intimate setting.

MASTER BEDROOM CORNER

Robert Jackson's artistry enhanced the master bedroom. He decoratively painted, in a corner of the room, a faux bookcase, concealing a door opening into a dressing area, and integrated it with an actual book-lined shelf on top of the arrangement. The profiles of the Queen Anne table and directoire chair, with its arms carved as winged maidens and apron decorated with architectural motifs, symbolized Hodgins's appreciation for uniquely shaped furniture.

MASTER BEDROOM FIREPLACE

A button-tufted armchair upholstered in off-white textured cotton, juxtaposed against a classically detailed French limestone fireplace mantel, composed a welcoming and comfortable setting for reading and relaxing. The inlaid Anglo-Indian and antique blackamoor side tables and the Gothic-style fire screen augmented the eclecticism in the bedroom.

MR. AND MRS. ALVIN ALLEN

Palm Beach, Florida, 1989

Alvin and Helaine Allen were longtime Boston-area clients of Hodgins's. Their apartment in Palm Beach was his third commission for them. Hodgins's interior decoration of the apartment was magical. He transformed fairly unremarkable space in a mid-1960s oceanfront building into a handsome tableau of pale colors, muted textures, and generous views of the Atlantic Ocean.

Hodgins first corrected the bones of the apartment. He plastered the popcorn ceiling, replaced the ordinary wood parquet floor with twenty-four-inch squares of honed travertine, and capitalized on a pair of existing structural columns that stood unadorned on the principal wall of the apartment. Because the columns could not be removed, Hodgins gave them integrity. He detailed them, and two false columns that he added along the same wall, with contemporary versions of classical capitals and bases. Together, the columns created "regularity, rhythm and a sense of architectural completeness," harmonizing with Hodgins's superlative interiors. In fact, when Hodgins finished the assignment for the Allens, Alvin Allen called him "to say how much he loved" the apartment.

CLOSEUP OF END TABLE

Hodgins accessorized the living room simply and elegantly. The grouping on one of the end tables included a rough travertine globe, a pot of freesias, and a classic column lamp. The varied patinas of the minimalist arrangement were amplified by the matchstick shades and the natural light filtering through them.

DINING ROOM

A pair of columns, with their classical detailing, framed a panoramic view of the ocean in the dining room. They also influenced Hodgins's design of the dining table. The marbleized table, which incorporated its own drawleaves, was supported by a double pedestal base emulating the columns. The regency-style chairs and their soft green leather upholstery were perfectly suited to the table.

LIVING ROOM

Hodgins achieved the pinnacle of "luxurious simplicity" in Mr. and Mrs. Allen's living room, offsetting it against the minimalist backdrop of matchstick window shades. He covered the sofa in natural canvas and maintained simplicity with the classic lacquered-parchment end tables he designed and the Karl Springer coffee table in goatskin.

Regency-style chairs with marbleized frames, gilded lion-head terminals, and claw feet contributed both elegance and originality to the setting. Their "slightly strong formal shape contrasted with the pale colors" of the living room.

VIEW TOWARD OCEAN

An expansive view of the ocean in the apartment set the precedent for Hodgins's neutral color scheme. He did not want the interior to overpower the rarefied setting. The daybed, which was also upholstered in natural canvas, organized and subdivided the combined living and dining room.

MR. AND MRS. FELIX ROHATYN

Southampton, New York, 1990

When Felix and Elizabeth Rohatyn purchased the two "park like" acres adjacent to their weekend house in Southampton, New York, they asked Hodgins to renovate and decorate the accompanying house, which had originally been a stable on a large estate. Initially, Mr. and Mrs. Rohatyn planned to use the cedar-shingled barnlike structure for a guesthouse. However, partway through the project, Mrs. Rohatyn decided, "without a word to her husband," to make the converted outbuilding, with "its openness and airy scale," their home. Mr. and Mrs. Rohatyn then turned their larger main house into the guesthouse, which Hodgins had also decorated.

The renovated stable, which *Architectural Digest* featured in the April 1993 issue, impressed Katharine Graham, publisher of *The Washington Post*. After Mrs. Graham read the article, she recommended to one of her sons who was building a summerhouse designed by Los Angeles architect Marc Appleton in Martha's Vineyard that he look at the photographs of the interiors, which she "considered ideal." Mr. Graham and his wife agreed. They hired Hodgins to decorate the house, which was also featured in the magazine.

ENTRANCE HALL

Hodgins "made a wide and welcoming entrance hall, keeping the sense that the building was originally a stable." He also restored the terra-cotta tile floor "where saddles were once racked." The nineteenth-century oval French country table, rustic English iron hall lantern, and antique American chest of drawers personalizing the stair landing were true to the unpretentiousness of the house.

LIVING ROOM

Hodgins worked with the help of senior designer Penny Matteson to make the tall-ceilinged living room "intimate, comfortable, and welcoming." Its two sitting areas, which were anchored by a pair of capacious Bielecky Brothers rattan sofas covered in natural cotton canvas, were oriented toward the fireplace. The mantel was particularly impressive. It was fabricated from three "simple [but substantial] lengths" of Indiana limestone and designed especially for the room. Oversized armchairs—neutrally upholstered—and small ottomans that "floated" on a herringbone-patterned sisal carpet spanning the entire room provided additional seating. The large draped octagonal table organized and separated the dining area from the living room.

DINING AREA

A pedestal dining table with a classic columnar base, specially designed by Hodgins to accommodate as many as fourteen guests, composed "a casual and comfortable dining area— good to look at and easy to use without completely overtaking the room." The rattan and rawhide-laced armchairs and country French serving cabinet blended into the relaxed setting enhanced by the "massive sliding [stable] doors" and iron bars that Hodgins "blackened to underline their presence." The painting of sunflowers hanging above the server is by Realist artist Polly Kraft.

MASTER BEDROOM

The first-floor master bedroom, which contained its own sitting room, fireplace, and bathroom, was decorated to give the interior a "gentle, old-fashioned" feeling. Rose-and-beige floral toile (favored by Mr. Rohatyn) dominated the bedroom. The enchanting material was used for the bed coverings, bed hangings, and a chair seat. Matchstick shades, white canvas curtains fringed in red cotton, and the tufted red-and-beige striped cotton ticking covering the bed bench complemented the all-over patterned décor.

MR. AND MRS. RALPH WILLARD

Boston, Massachusetts, 1990

In 1990, Ralph and Sherry Willard purchased a late-nineteenth-century brownstone in the center of Boston's Back Bay. The five-story house, which had been converted into ten apartments during the late 1940s, was being developed into three luxury condominiums when Mr. and Mrs. Willard purchased it. Fortunately, the original plans for the house existed at the Boston Building Department because the Willards planned to restore it to its original state. Hodgins, in collaboration with Lindsay Boutros-Ghali— the Boston architect—"knit [the house] back together." Their objective was to combine traditional craftsmanship with present-day living.

Originally, the Willards wanted the main floor off the entrance hall to be left open from the front to the back of the house. However, Boutros-Ghali suggested that round-headed arches outfitted with glazed doors partition the living room, dining room, and family room/kitchen, allowing versatility in the floor plan. To confirm the proposal, the contractor built a "dummy wall," which was moved back and forth until the size of the living room was determined. The walls throughout the house were painted white (Hodgins told Willard he could have any color he wanted as long as it was a shade of white), bleached oak floors were laid, and all the mantels, none of which were original to the house, were replaced, further unifying the interior. The existing wood molding was also enlarged "to give scale to the walls."

DINING ROOM ENTRANCE

An intimate seating area Hodgins created in a corner of the living room, with its sparely patterned and neutral-and-pastel-hued upholstery materials, contrasted with the strong color palette in the connecting dining room. Italian wool paisley from Clarence House, woven in colors of beige, brown, and turquoise, covered the dining table banquette and the Chippendale-style chairs were upholstered in Brunschwig & Fils blue strié velvet. The "park bench" green leather on the wingback chair also enriched the décor.

LIVING ROOM

Hodgins decorated the Willards' fourteen-foot-tall living room against the backdrop of an expansive bay window he and Robert Blankenship meticulously curtained and softly swagged in blue-green French silk taffeta, giving it the "air of a proscenium arch." The window drew natural light into the room, which reflected off the neutral and soft pastel upholstery material. The sofa was upholstered in off-white textured woven cotton and accented with pillows of silk taffeta striped on a bias in green and ivory. A "Hadley" chair covered in self-embroidered cream and pale gray cotton and a large tufted ottoman fronting the Louis XV–style fireplace, with its fringed herringbone-patterned spruce-green chenille upholstery, contributed additional restraint to the design scheme, which was weighted by a modicum of dark wood furniture.

DINING ROOM

The dining table was placed to one side of the dining room, enhancing flow between the three principal rooms on the main floor of the house. The softly bleached and stained herringbone-patterned floor and built-in cabinets and bookcases, which Hodgins likes to put in dining rooms as "it encourages people to talk and creates a pleasing informality," provided a classic and understated backdrop for the traditionally furnished room.

FAMILY ROOM/KITCHEN

Hodgins decorated the family room/kitchen with
linen material printed in floral-covered columns.
He upholstered the sofa and swagged the windows
in the tea ground material, complementing it with
brisbee curtains in unlined parchment cotton taffeta,
highback dining chairs covered with faded "Mono Blue
Roses" on a beige ground, and a pair of chairs covered
in ocean-blue textured cotton and embossed cocoa
wicker-weave leather. The family room/kitchen was
conducive to informal living and "quietly elegant."

MASTER BEDROOM

Taupe and cream chinoiserie linen toile was an
elegant backdrop for an eclectic arrangement of
furniture in the master bedroom, which Hodgins
designed to be "properly Bostonian in its understated
sense of period." The stripped pine and composition
mantel was eighteenth-century English and the
table placed in the bay window was Danish,
accompanied by a directoire-style open armchair. Plaid
patterned pillow and upholstery materials shaded
in beige, cream, ivory, and pale pink contributed
additional tone and texture to the room.

MR. WILLIAM HODGINS

Boston, Massachusetts, 1992

Bill Hodgins moved from his duplex apartment at 232 Clarendon Street to an eighteenth-floor condominium that was located nearby in the residential division of a Boston hotel. In downsizing and simplifying his life, he also gained wonderful services offered by the hotel and great views of Back Bay, the neighboring Charles River, and Cambridge.

Hodgins, who was accustomed to living in a late-nineteenth-century apartment with tall ceilings and elegant detailing, masterfully transformed the "bland" space of the new three-room apartment with classic moldings, tall baseboards, and the "brightest of eight white paint formulas in his repertoire" to create the illusion of larger and taller rooms. The creamy faux-concrete-tiled floors and the wall-to-wall windows in the apartment also helped him "fool the eye" while keeping "the contemporary feel of the apartment" and "a modern shell for [his] old things."

LIVING ROOM

Hodgins upholstered the oversized sofa and pair of matching armchairs in white cotton pique, melding them with the pale palette of the apartment and emphasizing the accompanying pieces of furniture and objects. He arranged the sitting area with a Louis XVI–style oval-back chair and a unique "table" composed of piled books made from papier-mâché. The Venetian-style Georgian mirror hanging above the sofa and the Swedish astrolabe, oversized antique globe, and barrel-back Russian chair augmented the originality of the comfortable grouping.

LIVING ROOM DESK CLOSEUP

Hodgins balanced the living room with a gray painted partner's desk he has moved from apartment to apartment. He treasures his compilation of unusual finds, including the small turn-of-the-century stool sitting deskside and the pedestaled marble ball specimen accessorizing the desk, which is identical to the model at Hodgins's house in Manchester. The large-scale nineteenth-century oil painting of two hunting hounds hanging above the armchair slides to reveal a built-in television.

LIVING ROOM TOWARD BOOKCASE

The built-in bookcase also contributed architectural integrity to the living room and displayed Hodgins's various collections, including Berlin faience garniture and bronzes from the seventeenth, eighteenth, and nineteenth centuries. The nineteenth-century portrait of the dog hanging in the center division of the cabinet, with its distinctive Edwardian frame, illustrates Hodgins's devotion to animals.

DINING AREA/ENTRANCE FOYER

Hodgins places a small round table in his entrance foyer when he entertains. The mirrored coat closet amplifies the corner and reflects the table with its singular pair of Italian side chairs with faux bois and gilded frames and a white painted Louis XVI-style chair upholstered in tête de negré leather. The rams' head table placed against the wall is Italian.

MASTER BEDROOM

Hodgins also decorated the master bedroom in a pale palette. He covered the floor in soft gray carpet, woven by Avena Carpets from England in an all-over pattern of ivory stars highlighted with a darker gray and he used striped linen ticking in similar hues for the upholstered headboard, bedskirt, and little Georgian-style settee at the foot of the bed. The bedroom derived contrast from the darkly stained and painted furniture and diverse artwork, including the pair of night tables that Hodgins designed and Robert Jackson decorated in black lacquered chinoiserie, and nude studies from Rudolf Nureyev's estate.

MR. AND MRS. FELIX ROHATYN

Cora, Wyoming, 1994

Hodgins's fourth project for Felix and Elizabeth Rohatyn was planning and decorating their western log house in Cora, Wyoming, in collaboration with local architects John and Nancy Carney. The house, which Mr. and Mrs. Rohatyn built from the ground up, was sited with Hodgins's perspective on an 800-acre working ranch that has been in the Carney family since they purchased it from the family of the original homesteaders during the early 1960s. John Carney's mother, Frederika Carney, is Elizabeth Rohatyn's sister.

The house is "large, but has the simplicity and warmth of an American country cabin" with exterior details and materials commensurate with its neighboring buildings, including square-cut corners and mortarless farmer's rock that runs along the foundation, overlays a bay in the screened porch, and forms all of the chimneys. The house was clustered with the other family ranch houses along the Upper Green River beneath the western slope of the Wind River Mountains. Hodgins's and the Carneys' objective "was to adapt the rough-hewn look of log homestead buildings to the needs of Mr. and Mrs. Rohatyn, whose lives are anything but rough-hewn." They also endeavored to make the house "sympathetic to the rest of the compound" as it aged.

GREAT ROOM

The principal wing of the house is a great room that includes the living room and dining room. It was decorated casually and, according to Felix Rohatyn, "to be as un-chichi as possible" and appropriate for relaxed family gatherings.

Walls of flattened hand-adzed pine logs, with "a soft, slightly driftwood look," composed the great room and offset the beamed and trussed cathedral ceiling that Hodgins painted white to reflect natural light filtering through windows incorporated into the sloped roof.

Hodgins oriented the seating in the great room toward a large sandstone fireplace. He upholstered the pair of "huge deep sofas" in quilted red-brushed cotton twill and accented them with cotton check and glazed chintz floral-patterned pillows in colors of red, burgundy, green, beige, and taupe. Country French–style armchairs with cushioned raffia seats and backs, eighteenth-century English and French country tables, and the outlining wrought-iron wall lights furthered the rusticity of the decor.

DINING AREA

Hodgins arranged raw birch Windsor dining chairs painted "bright, old, slightly worn red" and "meant for restaurant use" around a long and large trestle dining table made from antique white-oak French beams. The table was placed to take advantage of "the extraordinary views of landscape" framed by a series of windows spanning the principal wall of the great room. The red-and-white check canvas seat cushions on the chairs perpetuated the predominant color in the interior.

SCREENED PORCH

Hodgins furnished the screened porch comfortably. He built a substantial cushioned banquette into the expansive bay window overlooking the original 1930s homestead, 1940s barn, and the parts shop that was relocated to accommodate the new house. An oversized spindle-back bench and matching rocking chair—with frames of peeled logs and woven leather seats—and a porch swing requested by Mr. and Mrs. Rohatyn were also arranged in the screened room. The natural-and-white-dot jute pile carpet and floral-patterned canvas banquette pillows hand-painted in colors of white, soft gray, and caramel contributed to the rustic look.

MASTER BEDROOM

A wooden bed specially made with an unusually tall paneled headboard decorated in a vineyard motif anchored the master bedroom and offset whitewashed log walls that "differentiated [the bedroom] from the rest of the house." The rose, beige, and pumpkin floral-patterned quilt and matching euroshams dressing the bed softened the interior and embodied Mrs. Rohatyn's love of muted palettes.

MASTER BEDROOM AT BAY WINDOW

Natural light poured into the master bedroom through an expansive floor-to-ceiling bay window that captured a mesmerizing view of the mountains. An inviting upholstered chair covered in an oakleaf-patterned cotton and linen print and an oak drop-leaf table composed a comfortable setting within the extended floor plan.

MASTER BEDROOM SITTING AREA

Hodgins combined color, pattern, and texture in a corner of the sitting room against a pastoral backdrop dramatized by the Wind River Range. He covered the floor with a handwoven rag carpet, which integrated wool, chenille, linen, and cotton, and upholstered a tufted barrel-back armchair in multicolored floral-patterned linen. The sitting room proffered "a quiet, private place to read, work or have tea." In fact, the entire house evolved flawlessly from its inception because of Hodgins's comfortable relationship with his longstanding clients. He understood exactly how they lived.

PRIVATE RESIDENCE

Alexandria, Virginia, 1994

"Tranquility," derived from "shifting hues of off-white, soft putty, and stone" describes the interiors of a late-eighteenth-century house that William Hodgins decorated for a client in Alexandria, Virginia. The historic Colonial house, which was in need of restoration, was reworked on the exterior by architect Allan Greenberg. He "stripped the building of Victorian accretions, and designed a seamless, two-story, L-shaped addition," a garden and a pergola.

LIVING ROOM

Hodgins was inspired by the airiness and freshness of Russian and Scandinavian design when decorating the house in Alexandria. In the living room, he used a pale and powdery hued linen carpet and materials and predominantly whitewashed furniture, including the Swedish barrel-back armchairs that flanked the sofa. They were upholstered in finely ribbed lustrous silk taffeta. The highlight of the living room was Robert Jackson's floor-to-ceiling wall mural of a Tuscan landscape, which broadened the interior and complemented the curtain treatment in the bay window.

STUDIO TOWARD FIREPLACE

Hodgins's client has a certain style when it comes to choosing art. She confidently hung an oversized nineteenth-century Scottish landscape in the studio even though it "dwarfed" the sofa. The antiques mixing with "conventional" furnishings in the room included a rosewood table, a Louis XVI armchair, and a gilded regency mirror hanging above a French stone mantel chosen by Hodgins and his client "who had a [major] hand in the interiors."

STUDIO

Luxuriously upholstered furniture juxtaposed with aged pine floors retained in the renovation, and resourcefully restored and colonnaded walls inset with bookcases that Hodgins designed and added to the room, showed his sensitivity to the house's history. He harmonized subtly patterned chenille, silk damask, and gauffraged velvet materials with the qualities of late-eighteenth-century Colonial vernacular. Hodgins, in response to his client's wishes, and with a judicious use of white, also achieved subtle "nuances in temperature and texture, more than in hue, [that] become apparent with each change in light."

DINING ROOM

Hodgins anchored the delicately curtained dining room with an empire table, and surrounded it with mid-nineteenth-century French neoclassical side chairs and a banquette upholstered in narrowly striped ice-blue and gray woven silk. The complementing whitewashed and gilded Swedish chairs and an antique round English bookcase furthered the eclectic décor.

MASTER BEDROOM

Hodgins created a "range of textures and shades of white in the master bedroom [that was] as subtle as it [was] dramatic." He covered the floor with a pale gray wool carpet, woven by Avena Carpets in diagonally patterned, double-shadowed quatrefoils in shades of gray and cream. White silk taffeta, specially painted with sparkle dots by Peter Fasano, was used for the shirred headboard, lightly quilted bedspread, and bedskirt. The George II–style bench and Louis XVI–style chairs, with their very pale gilded soft old-world-white frames, ivory-white velvet, and fawn-and-ivory cotton upholstery, complemented the serene interior. The flower stand in front of the window was designed by Hodgins and painted by Yorke Kennedy.

MR. AND MRS. LEE DANIELS

Mashpee, Massachusetts, 1995

When Lee and Joan Daniels built a two-story classic contemporary house in Cape Cod, Massachusetts, they turned to William Hodgins for his highly valued guidance. Hodgins is not only a wonderful decorator; he also understands architecture, construction, and engineering. "Hodgins talks to architects, builders, and tradesmen in their own language" and convinces them "to do it his way, at his degree of precision and detail." He knows immediately what he wants, "labors over their work," and "pushes them to new heights. They in turn have enormous respect for Hodgins and learn from him."

Hodgins's "palette of soft, pretty colors," and generously proportioned furniture created a house for Mr. and Mrs. Daniels that is quiet, welcoming, and "supremely comfortable." Even one of their houseguests remarked, "This house makes you feel good."

LIVING ROOM

Although Mr. and Mrs. Daniels's living room and dining room were arranged within an open floorplan, Hodgins gave each area a sense of division. He placed a large sofa against the principal wall of the living room, accenting its beige-and-cream cotton upholstery with cotton pillows in bright solid yellow and sage green printed abstractly on a white ground.

Hodgins counterbalanced the grouping with parchment glazed parsons-style end tables and an oversized split-back chair covered in contemporary patterned natural cotton. The large coffee table, with its distinctive square legs, bun feet, and vibrant yellow glaze, gave additional appeal and uniqueness to the setting.

LIVING ROOM TOWARD DINING ROOM

Hodgins bordered the dining area with a second sofa, identically upholstered but slightly smaller than its counterpart. He also furnished the grouping with a cream lacquered coffee table and a pair of wicker club chairs, covering the cushions of the lattice-framed pieces in a neutral cotton-flax weave. The sofa pillows in solid blue and green woven raw silk exemplified Hodgins's good use of color.

DINING ROOM

Comfort and casualness were key in the dining room. Hodgins ordered extra-wide "Nantucket-style" armchairs with painted and lightly distressed frames. He upholstered their seats and backs in yellow-and-white woven cotton check.

Hodgins designed the dining table to be multipurposed. The pale parchment glazed rectangular table was composed of two square tables that sat on separate bases and were clipped together as one. The antique pine sideboard was nineteenth-century English. The resourceful configuration allowed Mr. and Mrs. Daniels to have seated dinners for six or eight or several rounds of bridge!

FAMILY ROOM

The soft blue color scheme in the family room embodied comfort and restfulness. Faded blue denim twill covered the upholstered furniture, their solid ground accented by pillows patterned in floral and geometric designs.

The graphic check in blue and ivory, the delicate patterns of blue roses, the fields of stripes in the rag carpet, and the white cotton pinpoint curtains all contributed character to the interior. However, it was the pillow in clear yellow cotton that was the highpoint. Its dynamic and complementary hue empowered the monochromatic color scheme in the room.

MR. AND MRS. LEE MUNDER

Palm Beach, Florida, 1995

Laura Munder was so truly in awe of Hodgins's work "and respected what he represented" that she insisted Lee sell his vintage 1967 Silver Shadow Rolls Royce to pay for two Delta/Urban sofas. That was in 1988, the year Lee and Laura hired Hodgins for the first time to decorate their home in Bloomfield Hills, Michigan. Laura had met Hodgins several years earlier through Linda Taubman, her sister.

The Munders' relationship with Hodgins flourished. By 1995, he had completed three houses for them and an office for Mr. Munder. The 1995 commission was the Munders' second collaboration with Hodgins in Palm Beach. It too included the Delta/Urban sofas that they still have to this day!

John Volk designed Mr. and Mrs. Munder's oceanfront British Colonial for Henry Ford II during the late 1940s. They purchased the very grand house from its second owners in 1995. Mrs. Munder said "it needed everything," a complete transformation from its "very old-world, formal" vestige into a home that functioned for a modern family. Hodgins, along with notable Palm Beach architect Jeff Smith who oversaw the extensive remodeling of the house, accomplished the heady task.

LIVING ROOM

Hodgins devoted a great deal of time to correcting the bones of the house and giving it "strong architecture." In the living room, he specified tall baseboards and a sixteen-inch-deep cornice with arched French doors breaking into it. The masterful detailing "made the [oceanfront] room seem taller and more elegant."

The existing oak floors that were "very, very deeply stained dark brown" and modeled on the floors in Bill Blass's New York apartment also weighted the living room and embraced the large-scale furniture and beguiling antiques that Mr. and Mrs. Munder acquired at auction and during their shopping trips with Hodgins. In London, they found the early nineteenth-century regency mahogany desk that was centered in the living room and organized it into three sitting areas. They also procured a pair of early twentieth-century Near Eastern ottomans, a nineteenth-century Indian ivory inlaid table, and a set of four late-eighteenth-century Italian grisaille tondo paintings, all perfectly placed by Hodgins as if they had always been there.

Muted colors and subtle textures relaxed the significance of the antiques and toned down the formality of the living room. Hodgins chose natural striped linen and ivory textured woven cotton for the sofas and armchairs. He also used colors of soft blue, seafoam, and jade in velvet and various silk materials, drawing them from his customary palette and a collection of frosted sea glass–like cosmetic bottles that Laura sent him for inspiration. "This was how she wanted the house to feel."

LOGGIA

French linen patterned in sprays of roses and wisteria covered most of the furniture in the loggia and infused very quiet colors throughout the interior. Soft rose, blue, and green, and muted earth tones, printed on cream ground, created the English country look—an approach unanticipated in Palm Beach décor and attained with great care by Hodgins and his clients. The loggia was a room for dining, relaxing, and playing games. The sitting area was centered along a principal wall of contiguous arched French doors opening to the pool loggia. The comfortable grouping was offset by an oval mahogany Spanish dining table and game table placed on opposite sides of the room. The dining table was large and it sat in tandem with an equally capacious banquette upholstered in tufted cream leather. Oversized rattan chairs, with cushions fabricated in the French linen, completed the seating arrangement at the table.

LOGGIA CARD TABLE

The card table was especially unusual. Its top of inlaid antique marble augmented the organic elements in the room, especially the geometric-patterned tumbled-stone floor. The pair of French doors aligned with the table give a view into the pool loggia.

POOL LOGGIA

Hodgins had the "luxury of ordering furniture from Morocco" for the Munders' pool and ocean loggias. The intensive renovation of the house allowed for the prolonged time it took to make and deliver to Palm Beach the exotic pieces Hodgins admired during his excursions to that part of the world.

A grouping of Moroccan furniture composed the sitting area in the pool loggia. The unusually carved and intricately fretted settee and armchairs were painted soft gray-blue to simulate sun-faded color. The rusticity and informality of the setting was advanced by the preweathered teak ladder-back dining chairs and stone-capital tables from Michael Taylor Designs.

MS. SALLY PINGREE

Washington, D.C., 1997

Sally Pingree is a longstanding client of Hodgins's. The commission in 1997 marked her second one with him in the District of Columbia. It also followed projects in Boston and in Maryland—on the Chesapeake Bay. Ms. Pingree asked Hodgins to look at the present house when she considered purchasing it. He had always admired Ms. Pingree's "taste and style," including the appeal of the classic and "graceful" Georgian-style house built in 1926.

DINING ROOM BANQUETTE

Hodgins arranged an intimate sitting area
in the dining room. He placed a tufted
banquette into a corner of the room with a
diminutive nineteenth-century regency black
lacquer and simulated-bamboo table.
The banquette was particularly beautiful. It was
luxuriously upholstered in Scalamandré green silk
damask and accented with flame stitch-patterned
pillows in Clarence House green cut velvet from
France. The Louis XVI–style wall lights, with
their acorn finials, reinforced the grouping.

ENTRANCE HALL

Hodgins "amplified moldings and added cornices"
to the house, including in the entrance hall where he
designed a stenciled pattern for the wood floor. Malcolm
Robson, the English master grainer and marbler,
executed the handsome work in many color stains. He
also "softly marbleized" the walls. The antiques in the
hall included the eighteenth-century country table and
oxblood-glazed sang de boeuf vase mounted as a lamp.

LIVING ROOM TOWARD FIREPLACE

An eighteenth-century French limestone mantel offset a generously proportioned ottoman and a pair of oversized Louis XVI–style chairs covered in luxuriant Clarence House sapphire blue velvet. The ottoman, which Hodgins upholstered in Scalamandré multicolored striped material and skirted in soft blue and white bullion fringe, enhanced the touches of tender color in the interior. The régence-style wall lights flanking the fireplace were among the understated accents Hodgins placed in the living room.

LIVING ROOM

An antique floral-patterned Bessarabian carpet patterned in impressionistic colors underscored the living room and its arrangement of fine antiques and luxuriously upholstered furniture. Hodgins hung a Louis XV–style giltwood mirror above the principal sofa, which he covered in Scalamandré antique white damask and accented with silk taffeta and antique needlepoint pillows. The seating area also included a Louis XV mahogany and brass inlaid bouillotte table and a cream lacquered coffee table from France. Hodgins purposely left the arched windows bare for their classic beauty and the diffusion of natural light.

LIBRARY

Walls faux grained by Malcolm Robson instilled warmth and comfort in the library and harmonized with the Chinese needlepoint carpet covering the floor. The carpet was particularly handsome. Its cocoa-brown ground, geometric circular motifs, and floral designs in reds, greens, blues, and ochres influenced the color palette in the room.

Various materials and textures, including oxblood chenille, tobacco leather, and floral chintz, also contributed richness to the library. The chintz, which covered a split-back chair, fireside ottoman, and a pair of pillows on the sofa, fortified the English country look.

DINING ROOM

The dark polished George III dining table and its Louis XVI–style chairs covered in black leather glowed against the backdrop of a Portuguese needlepoint carpet and pale yellow walls. Yellow, which Hodgins favors for its warmth and sunny qualities, also complemented the large English regency convex mirror and its distinctive parcel gilt and faux-bronze circular frame. The intricately carved and gray painted demilune console under the mirror is Louis XVI.

SUNROOM

Garden ambiance prevailed in Hodgins's decoration of Sally Pingree's sunroom. The pair of sofas covered with French linen patterned in sprays of roses and wisteria unifed the relationship between the indoors and the outdoors.

Hodgins incorporated additional elements in the sunroom that conveyed an out-of-doors spirit. He surfaced the coffee table in Italian tile and accented the interior with multiple shades of green, including the set of Windsor dining chairs decoratively painted by Fred Browne.

MASTER BEDROOM

Hodgins decorated Ms. Pingree's bedroom to echo her lush garden. He added the circular window, French doors, and balcony, and used copiously decorated floral chintz in the design scheme. Hand-painted furniture and materials in shades of white and pale blue also instilled airiness within the light-filled interior and complemented the antique American bed.

GUEST BEDROOM

Hodgins created a virtual paradise for Sally Pingree's guests. He decorated the guest bedroom principally in dauphine blue-and-white floral toile, covering the walls and dressing the windows and bed in the enchanting material. The toile, with the bespoke carpet woven by Avena Carpets, also enhanced the diverse arrangement of antiques in the bedroom, which included an eighteenth-century Italian commode, a Queen Anne walnut table and regency, and American painted side chairs.

197

MR. AND MRS. BRIAN KNEZ

Weston, Massachusetts, 1999

Brian and Debra Knez commissioned Hodgins to redecorate the white clapboard Colonial-style house that they built in 1993. The house, which was designed by Judge Skelton Smith, the Boston architecture firm, is a contemporary interpretation of vernacular New England architecture. Its considerable footprint and skillful fenestration presented Hodgins with pleasing, light-filled interiors that overlooked two acres of verdant surroundings.

LIVING ROOM AT PAINTING

Hodgins chose eclectic seating in the living room. He paired a sofa with an iron ball coffee table and used a moderately distressed wooden gateleg table for an end table. The pair of burled-wood Russian chairs and Han pottery lamps preserved the symmetry in the arrangement.

LIVING ROOM AT WINDOW

Hodgins decorated Mr. and Mrs. Knez's living room in plan with its engaging vistas. He chose neutral colors and luxurious textures, integrating the bucolic landscape and its natural colors with his own masterful design.

Silk taffeta curtains in ivory composed a beautiful view of the outdoors and offset a singular arrangement of eclectic furniture: the contemporary goatskin coffee table, the French three-tiered walnut end table designed by Rose Tarlow, and the antique burled-wood Russian barrel-back chair, each of which were augmented by the handsomely designed and appointed sofa. The striped pillow was needlepointed by Debra's mother.

DINING ROOM CLOSEUP

Hodgins unified his eclectic arrangement of furniture and accessories in the dining room with classically designed models. The bow-fronted cabinet, the Louis XVI–style chair, and ceramic Chinese lamp, although contemporary, referenced history.

DINING ROOM

Hodgins furnished the dining room with a handmade Abadjian carpet and emphasized several of its accent colors in the Bordeaux leather and woven cotton check covering the outside backs of the Louis XVI–style dining chairs and the stationary curtains of beige-and-cream striped silk.

Hodgins maintained lightness and airiness in the room. He specified natural sycamore for the dining table and pair of bow-fronted cabinets, and screened the expansive window with sheer silk café curtains. Hodgins's unwavering sensitivity to natural light throughout Mr. and Mrs. Knez's house was the essence of its design.

MR. AND MRS. JULIAN COHEN

Palm Beach, Florida, 2002

In 2002, Julian and Carol Cohen purchased a three-bedroom condominium in Palm Beach. The apartment, which was contiguous with the condominium Mrs. Cohen still owned, but had purchased in 1986 with Norman Feinberg, her late husband, enabled Mr. and Mrs. Cohen to incorporate the two residences and create interiors commensurate with the nearby house from which they were moving. Fortunately, Julian and Carol Cohen had the ideal team to accomplish their task. Together, William Hodgins, architect Richard Sammons—a principal of the firm Fairfax & Sammons—and Jim Woolems reconfigured, renovated, and integrated the new space with Mrs. Cohen's original home, and, with each of their respective talents, created one of the most outstanding and distinguished apartments in the heart of Palm Beach.

ENTRANCE FOYER

An elliptical and classically detailed entrance foyer foreshadowed the elegance and understatement of Mr. and Mrs. Cohen's apartment. The foyer floor, which was configured in the Marie Antoinette pattern, was paved in bleached and pickled white oak and inlaid diagonally with a windowpane design of naturally finished walnut. A narrow band of the inset wood outlined the perimeter of the floor to finish the meticulously executed design inspired by a classical French aesthetic.

Hodgins furnished the entrance foyer with choice antiques. He juxtaposed a nineteenth-century regency oak center table against a softly shaped camel-back banquette, lusciously upholstered in a butterscotch-and-cream woven stripe material made by Leni's Inc. The stylishly bold upholstery of the seating also complemented the Italian white painted and giltwood commode and Louis XVI carved and gilded French mirror, both dating to the eighteenth century.

LIVING ROOM AT FIREPLACE CLOSEUP

The aggregation of antiques at the sitting area alongside the fireplace was particularly notable, including the exceptionally rare early eighteenth-century Queen Anne pier glass mirror hanging above the mantel. The Italian mahogany tea table, with its distinctive barley-twist legs and detailing in gold leaf, completed the space.

LIVING ROOM

Luxuriant materials, including ivory silk damask, textured ivory cotton and linen, and ivory-and-beige striped silk taffeta distinguished the principal sitting area in the living room. The neutral hues of the tableau were restful and they acquiesced gracefully to the accents of spare colors infused by the Italian silk damask of the Louis XV fauteuil and the embroidered and fringed silk pillow on the sofa.

LIVING ROOM AT SERVER

Hodgins anchored the principal wall in the living room with a classically detailed server that he designed and had decoratively painted warm white with soft highlights and a softly marbleized base. He accessorized the cabinet adroitly, arranging it with a Chinese sewing box and a pair each of diminutive French porcelain cachepots and French gilt bronze ormolu candlesticks that were mounted as lamps. The flanking Italian Louis XVI-style chairs were painted, gilded, and upholstered in spare floral-patterned lampas brocade by Scalamandré.

LIVING ROOM AT FIREPLACE

Hodgins furnished the sizeable living room with two seating areas. He placed an intimate grouping alongside the eighteenth-century Louis XV limestone mantel. Elegant upholstery materials, including the ivory silk damask covering the sofa and armchair and the toast-colored cut-velvet leaf design on the pair of eighteenth-century Louis XVI painted armchairs, embodied the quietness of Hodgins's interiors. The understated materials allowed the shapes and singularity of the antiques to resonate discreetly throughout the room.

ALCOVE CLOSEUP

Textured materials and painted finishes distinguished the alcove, which, like the living room, was carpeted in a Tibetan wool and silk carpet. Its colors in soft tones of ivory and beige harmonized with the hand-quilted pale-white-on-beige Fortuny covering the sofa, and the oversized split-back chairs, which were upholstered in plush beige chenille. The ecru French crackle lacquer finish on the coffee table, which contrasted effectively with the highly polished end tables, contributed character to the room.

ALCOVE

The living room transitioned naturally into the less formal alcove, a bookcase-lined library that was decorated in neutral tones and appointed with rare antiques, Chinese Export porcelains, and contemporary art. The eclectic mélange included a grouping of Hans Hoffman India ink drawings on handmade paper, English mahogany and brass end tables, and pair of important late-eighteenth-century Louis XV fauteuils en chassis arranged at the forefront of the room.

DINING ROOM

Significant English antiques, soft hues of blue, green, and ivory, and luxurious silk taffeta composed a superlatively elegant and magnificent dining room. The classically detailed interior glowed with the richness of the mahogany finish of the late-eighteenth-century Sheraton serpentine sideboard and regency two-pillar dining table, which correspondingly highlighted the distressed old-world white frames of the Louis XVI–style dining chairs and their bone leather upholstery. Additional sparkle came from the late-eighteenth-century Swedish cut-glass-and-gilt-bronze chandelier with its lower tier plateau of medium-blue glass purchased at H. M. Luther Antiques in New York—one of Hodgins's favored antiquarians.

FAMILY ROOM

Hodgins underscored the family room, which was originally the living room in Mrs. Cohen's apartment, with cream-colored textures and sparely infused colors. He covered the floor in wool carpet and upholstered the furniture in silk chenille. The pair of fringed ivory silk damask pillows on the sofa, and the floral French linen pillow, with its tender shades of pink, green, rose, and bone, expressed the subtleties of Hodgins's decorating and also synchronized flawlessly with Helen Frankenthaler's 1982 oil painting, "Bayside."

MASTER BEDROOM SITTING AREA

Hodgins organized and arranged the sitting
area against a backdrop of soft-blue, textured
curtains. Although he modeled and fringed the
valance of the window treatment to correspond
with the bed canopy, the departure from the
Cumming's chintz at the window, and the skilled
placement of a split-back upholstered chair,
gave the sitting area its own sense of place.

The sitting area was distinguished by neutral
textures. Hodgins upholstered the love seat and
offsetting armchair in ecru cotton and linen and
skirted both pieces with ivory bullion fringe. The
fringed chintz pillows on the love seat and the faux
shagreen coffee table enhanced the cohesiveness of
the combined bedroom/sitting room.

MASTER BEDROOM

Hodgins created a beautifully picturesque
master bedroom when he first decorated the
apartment for Mrs. Cohen. He dressed the bed
and fashioned its gathered and fringed canopy
and shirred upholstered headboard with Rose
Cumming's "Lace," "an enchanting pale-blue
glazed cotton chintz patterned in off-white
swags of lace embracing stylized bouquets of
multicolored roses and fuchsia in each of its
respective bows." Classic pieces of French-style
furniture, each one hand-painted and superbly
detailed and decorated, restrained botanicals by
Basilius Besler, and a notable collection of soft-
blue-and-white English Coalport were perfect
accompaniments to the bedroom arrangement
that remains unchanged to this day.

PRIVATE RESIDENCE

Alexandria, Virginia, 2002

In 1916, Washington, D.C. architect William Webster designed and built a summer cottage for himself on the banks of the Potomac River. The charming white clapboard Edwardian-style house, which stood "on a piece of land that was originally part of George Washington's farm," was purchased as a weekend home by Hodgins's client in 2002. Although the historic cottage was geographically close to her principal residence, spiritually, it was "a world away." She loved driving "down the bumpy dirt road that [led] to the house." She felt as if she "could be in New England."

Hodgins, with the help of design assistants Gregory Richardson and Garrow Kedigian, simplified the interior of the cottage. He removed "walls that had [closed] up the downstairs rooms," opening the living room, dining room, and breakfast area to each other and amplifying views of the river. "Existing windows and doors were replaced by almost floor-to-ceiling French windows and doors," allowing more light into the interior. "Classic cornices and moldings were added, and the first-floor ceilings were raised fourteen inches."

ENTRANCE HALL

In the entrance hall, a mixture of French antiques, a lustrous jade-green Chinese porcelain lamp, and organic elements melded harmoniously against the backdrop of classic details. The mahogany table, gilded partition mirror, and leather-upholstered French régence wing chair, spanning in provenance between the early eighteenth and middle twentieth centuries, were downplayed by the casualness of a bamboo basket and fully shuttered windows. The English wallpaper, patterned with soft-blue polka dots on a cream ground, stood out in contrast to the shiny dark-stained walnut floor.

LIVING ROOM

Hodgins's client "loves [gentle] colors more than anyone
[he's] ever worked for." White walls, white sheer linen
curtains, and cotton and linen upholstery materials subtly
patterned in allover floral and oakleaf designs and printed
in colors of the palest gray and cream created etherealness in
the living room and harmonized with its tranquil views of
the Potomac River. A unique mixture of furniture, including
the off-white Nantucket table with tassel apron designed by
Rose Tarlow, empire walnut swivel chair with scrolled arms,
and antique triangular English étagère placed alongside
the tufted blue leather sofa, individualized the décor.

DINING AREA

Natural light poured into the dining room through a wall of half-shuttered French windows and illuminated the quiet colors, unique objects, and rich dark wood and painted finishes. The oval walnut dining table was surrounded by Rose Tarlow Chippendale-style chairs painted old-world white, slightly distressed and slipcovered in seafoam textured cotton. Fanciful carved antique corbels supporting a painted and marble-topped wooden shelf designed by Hodgins and the pedestaled American gate finials from a fence in Maine, with their original "uneven" flaking paint, appealed both to him and his client "for their shape" and aged patina.

DINING AREA CLOSEUP

Hodgins arranged a corner of the dining room with an intimate sitting area, anchored by a Chippendale-style sofa he slipcovered in an allover floral design, printed in cream on a pale-gray cotton ground. The beautiful English material, which carried over from the living room, maintained the consistency of design between the two rooms. The nineteenth-century English orangery chair, painted old-world white and glazed in beige, was another "special" find that had been with Hodgins's client for many years. She found it in Boston during the late 1970s, when they first met and he decorated her "tiny apartment" in Back Bay.

SITTING/BREAKFAST AREA

In the sitting/breakfast area, which was off the living room, Hodgins placed a regency rosewood and bronze circular center table against the backdrop of classically detailed built-in bookcases and a Louis XVI-style stone fireplace mantel he designed. The Niermann Weeks Italian-style armchairs surrounding the table, with their carved and old-world-white painted frames and subtly patterned linen upholstery, symbolized Hodgins's fondness for combining light and dark finishes.

MASTER BEDROOM

Subdued colors of celadon and cream in the narrow-striped cotton wallcovering and "filmy, dreamlike" sheer white linen curtains composed a restful and light-filled master bedroom, and highlighted the views of the Potomac River. The Travers floral bouquet print of the duvet and shams, with its shades of soft yellow, greens, and white on a pale-rose linen ground, complemented the late-eighteenth-century iron, tole, and bronze English bed that was without hangings, "to emphasize its architectural character."

MR. AND MRS. EDWARD HYMAN JR.

New York, New York, 2002

Edward and Caroline Hyman originally commissioned Hodgins in 2000 to decorate the vernacular shingle-sided beach house they were building on the tip of Fire Island. Mrs. Hyman had always followed and admired Hodgins's work, which she saw in magazines. Because she and her husband were parents of young children, they hesitated using him due to his pale palette. However, when Mr. and Mrs. Hyman began the project on Fire Island, Mrs. Hyman hired Hodgins, telling him "to just do it!" She also asked Hodgins for architectural guidance. He gave her a lot to think about, including the type of windows to use and showed her how they would look according to plans drawn by Garrow Kedigian—a design assistant in Hodgins's office.

When the Fire Island house was completed, Mr. and Mrs. Hyman asked Hodgins to work on the living room and dining room and their childrens' bedrooms in their Upper East Side apartment. They also asked him to fine-tune other rooms in the duplex apartment, including the master bedroom and guest bedroom.

LIVING ROOM

Hodgins arranged the principal seating in the living room before an imposing view of the East River. He placed the sofa, which was upholstered in ivory damask, between a pair of luxuriously curtained windows and highlighted it with a skirt trimmed in ivory chenille and pillows in celadon silk taffeta and rose-colored textured silk. The flanking Austrian burled-wood and English black lacquer octagonal tables and pair of major Georgian-style Gainsborough open armchairs reinforced the symmetrical grouping.

LIVING ROOM CLOSEUP

Hodgins filled the living room with soft colors and subtle textures. He specified a Stark Carpet contemporary wool Aubusson, handwoven in a wool cut-loop pile and specially colored in soft blue and ivory and curtained the windows with alternating striped panels of beige and ivory silk taffeta that were seamed together. The green silk damask on the tufted ottoman and Lee Jofa cream linen covering the pair of Gainsborough armchairs, with its exotic "bird-and-branch" pattern in colors of pale blue, mauve, rose, and violet, embodied the restraint of Hodgins's decorating.

LIVING ROOM CLOSEUP

Hodgins weighted the pale color scheme in the living room with distinctive antiques. He placed a French empire mahogany gueridon with a brass gallery, brass inlay, and three black lacquered animal form legs alongside a chair covered in tufted ivory textured silk and a sofa upholstered identically to its counterpart. The subtleness of the French ivory glazed crackle linen finish on the coffee table, ivory crackle glaze on the Christopher Spitzmiller lamps, and floral brocade pillow accenting the chair were highlights of the understated interior.

DINING ROOM

Hodgins underscored the dining room with a Steven King hand-knotted wool Agra carpet and emphasized several of its accent colors in the camel leather and mauve cotton check covering the Louis XVI–style dining chairs and the glazed aquamarine walls and silk taffeta curtains. The Louis XVI oval dining table, George III cut-glass chandelier that Mrs. Hyman purchased at Sotheby's auction of the collection of Patricia Kluge, and Louis XVI white marble fireplace mantel from A & R Asta Ltd in New York harmonized flawlessly with the Georgian-style detailing Hodgins conceived with the help of Richard Burke, a Boston-area architectural designer.

PRIVATE RESIDENCE

McLean, Virginia, 2004

Bill Hodgins, along with architect Richard Sammons, worked carefully to give the new white clapboard Colonial Revival house that their client bought in McLean, Virginia, "a sense of tradition, of belonging." They designed all the moldings and chair rails and added two more arched doorways to the existing sequence of two, creating an enfilade of the conservatory, living room, hallway, and dining room. Hodgins also painted the cornices in the house "so they glow[ed]," enhancing their presence.

ENTRANCE HALL

In the entrance hall, the faux marbre tile floor painted by Franklin Tartaglione, the fine decorative painter, created a light, airy, and natural backdrop for dark wood antiques, including the late-nineteenth-century mahogany table Hodgins placed against the white paneled wainscoting, further highlighting his desired contrast of classic and distinctive shapes with neutral tones. The early eighteenth-century French régence wing chair, with its original gauffrage leather, and gilded French partition mirror hanging above the table contributed additional character to the hall.

LIVING ROOM TOWARD CONSERVATORY

A consecutive pair of arched doorways created enfilade between the conservatory and living room. The living room, which was arranged with traditional antiques, including the rosewood and bronze center table, and English regency demilune mahogany bookcase and its replica flanking the fireplace, and a pair of Louis XVI chairs, contrasted with the adjoining windowed and casually furnished conservatory. The antique pine garden cabinet standing at the entrance to the light-filled room was designed by Hodgins and highlighted with botanicals painted by the decorative artist Emilie Henry.

LIVING ROOM

Hodgins's client, who says that "beige is a bright color to [me]," worked closely with him to attain the restful hues and textures responsive to her good taste. In the living room, the windows were curtained in unlined creamy beige silk taffeta and the walls were painted pale linen white—a finish that Hodgins says ages well. The upholstery materials were also restrained. Off-white silk chenille covered the sofa and beige woven linen damask was specified for the pair of split-back chairs.

Contrast was important to Hodgins's decoration of the living room. The Agra carpet shaded in cream, beige, honey, and the palest shades of pink and gray was highlighted against the exposed ebonized wood floor, and the round Biedermeier table placed in front of the window, with its "slightly strong formal [shape]," reinforced Hodgins's penchant for juxtaposing dark finishes with light colors.

LIVING ROOM CLOSEUP

The arched doorway opening into the living room framed a view of an intimate sitting area set against a relaxed backdrop of diaphanous linen sheers and silk taffeta curtains. The small sofa and split-back chair, which were upholstered in beige linen damask, emanated pure comfort. The grouping was complemented by the regency-style coffee table and flanking pair of whitewashed Swedish barrel-back armchairs.

CONSERVATORY

Hodgins decorated the conservatory in consonance with the surrounding landscape created by Peter Cummin, the highly respected garden designer. Hodgins specified off-white limestone for the floor and painted the walls and ceiling white, disseminating natural light throughout the seven-sided room. The upholstered chair and sofa pillows covered in wisteria-printed English chintz introduced subtle shades of rose, pink, and beige to the décor.

LIBRARY

Celadon strié walls glazed by Marcus Pluntke, the northern Virginia painter, created a restful backdrop for Hodgins's interior decoration of the library. He anchored the room with a very deep sofa that he purchased at Sotheby's auction of the estate of Bill Blass. The sofa, reupholstered in green strié linen velvet and trimmed with bullion fringe, contrasted handsomely with the celadon-and-ivory English toile curtains and armchair upholstery, printed in silhouettes of ladies and gentlemen. The Turkish-style carpet, shaded in soft green, blue, caramel, and cocoa, added restrained accents of color and pattern to the interior.

DINING ROOM

Hodgins decorated the dining room with a neutral palette of pearl silk taffeta curtains and off-white crosshatched walls glazed by Marcus Pluntke, complementing the noncolors with varied hues of soft blue and green. A Steven King Tibetan area carpet, with a celadon ground and floral motif subtly patterned in ivory, covered the floor. Painted and slightly distressed Chippendale-style dining chairs, designed by Rose Tarlow and upholstered in slate-blue strié velvet, surrounded an oval Italian walnut table with handsome Baroque-style turned legs. The mid-nineteenth-century mahogany banquette, which was decoratively painted and upholstered in sea-green damask, contributed character to the interior.

DINING ROOM CLOSEUP

Hodgins is a master of interior architecture. "A lot of people come to [his] firm for [that reason.]" In the present house, he detailed the arched doorways on the first floor with an outlining band of wooden pearls, and in the dining room, he incorporated the imaginative motif in a smaller scale along the chair rail and cornice. The Georgian-style lead crystal chandelier from Nesle, Inc. and rose-colored hurricane lamps offsetting the floral centerpiece on the dining table sparkled, giving the interior additional patina.

FAMILY ROOM CLOSEUP

Hodgins placed a tufted chaise longue upholstered in a softly shaded and patterned oakleaf print alongside the fireplace, providing a comfortable setting for reading and relaxing. The antique French mantel, with its aged limestone patina, highlighted the appeal and character of the room.

FAMILY ROOM

A pitched ceiling designed by Richard Sammons and paneled walls faux painted in walnut by Marcus Pluntke distinguished the family room from the other rooms in the house. The dark paneling gave Hodgins an effective background for the pale-hued materials, textures, and surfaces he used to create a warm and comfortable room. He covered the floor with a subtly textured and grid-patterned Tibetan area carpet, its shades of ivory and soft blue highlighting the tufted sofa upholstered in soft-blue leather. The Italian end table with its "strong carved legs" and "awkward-looking [lions' paw] feet" and the parchment-covered card table with its Niermann Weeks Italian-style armchairs contributed eclecticism to the arrangement.

MASTER BEDROOM

Hodgins "finds white the most comforting color for a bedroom." In the present master bedroom, he used "fine gradations of white." The curtains were made from snowy silk taffeta, the carpet was white-on-white linen in a damask pattern, and the muted wall mural was a pastoral landscape painted en grisaille by Franklin Tartaglione. The pale-blue velvet on the parcel gilt bench placed at the foot of the bed enhanced the restful interior.

BEDROOM CORNER

The painted Louis XV–style bergère and ottoman, with its celery-green chenille upholstery, enlivened a corner of the bedroom. The Louis XVI–style gray painted bouillotte table with its bronze detailing and tierettes individualized the arrangement of furniture.

MR. AND MRS. STEPHEN WEINER

Boston, Massachusetts, 2004

William Hodgins's triumph for Mr. and Mrs. Stephen Weiner at their Back Bay penthouse in Boston took his consistently excellent work to new heights. Hodgins's ability to create outstanding interiors in the same apartment twice, initially for Julian and Eunice Cohen, and then twenty-three years later for Stephen and Roberta Weiner, is but a fine example of his superb taste, resourcefulness, and connoisseurship.

ENTRANCE HALL

Hodgins decorated Mr. and Mrs. Weiner's entrance hall against the backdrop of classic crown moldings designed for their apartment by architects Alfred Wojciechowski and David Ferris of the Boston firm CBT/Childs Bertman Tseckares. Wojciechowski's and Ferris's elegant detailing in the hall, and throughout the entire apartment, welcomed luxuriously upholstered furniture and museum-quality antiques that Hodgins perceptively advised his clients to acquire, including, for the hall, a late eighteenth-century Louis XVI commode with gilt bronze hardware and sabots and a George II giltwood mirror purchased at H.M. Luther Antiques. The early eighteenth-century hexagonal enameled censer accessorizing the commode exemplifies the rare and distinctive Chinese porcelains collected by Mr. and Mrs. Weiner.

LIVING ROOM CLOSEUP

The early nineteenth-century empire armchair, with its exotic and sumptuous silk velvet upholstery from Brunschwig & Fils, was key to the decoration of the living room. The chair form echoed the public garden below: the view of the legendary swan boats is one of the coveted panoramas that Mr. and Mrs. Weiner enjoy from their terrace.

LIVING ROOM OVERVIEW
(PREVIOUS PAGES)

Mrs. Weiner "wanted a very pale apartment" with "a white living room." Hodgins gave it to her "without trepidation," asking the painter "to keep mixing until the white wasn't simply white but white white white." Hodgins also stained the floors deep brown, thereby intensifying the purity of the white and making it weightier.

Hodgins underscored the living room with a white wool carpet from Stark Carpet, patterned with free-flowing vines, and arranged the light-filled interior with two sitting areas. He upholstered the furniture primarily in white woven linen and pearl-colored velvet, and fortified the frothy colored materials against pale-blue suede and aquamarine cut velvet covering the antique regency and empire armchairs interspersed throughout the room. The stationary curtains of white silk taffeta, with their shirred headings and pavé chenille trim, resonated with Mrs. Weiner's design sensibilities.

Hodgins anchored the secondary sitting area from the balancing bay that extended the forefront of the living room toward the terrace. The light-filled division enlivened the inherently pure hues of the white woven linen covering the sofa and button-tufted chair and the pearl-colored cut velvet on the upholstered chair. The pale-aqua-and-ivory silk brocade pillows on the sofa sustained the subtle infusion of the palest hues of blue in the room.

LIVING ROOM

Hodgins arranged the principal seating in the living room against the backdrop of Mr. and Mrs. Weiner's beautifully landscaped wraparound limestone terrace and the dramatic, unobstructed views of the Boston skyline. He offset a tufted rolled-arm sofa with two Biedermeier pedestal side tables and a contemporary low coffee table finished in French blanc-ecru crackled lacquer. The pair of exquisite Scalamandré lampas brocade pillows on the sofa—sparely patterned in stylized flowers and plumes shaded in aqua, turquoise, and ivory—infused subtle colors into the design scheme.

LIVING ROOM AT COMMODE

A fine and unusual Swedish neoclassical gilt
bronze and brass mahogany commode paired
with a compilation of works on paper by master
artists, including Matisse and Pissarro, composed
a pedigreed arrangement alongside the fireplace.
The restfulness of the textured white carpet and
the white woven linen upholstery covering the
button-tufted chair ensured the late-eighteenth-
century antique cabinet—one of the judicious
acquisitions that Hodgins recommended his
clients purchase from H. M. Luther Antiques—
its appropriate sense of place in the grouping.

LIVING ROOM BAY

A classic late-nineteenth-century Louis XVI
bureau plat and a hand-painted and gilded empire
armchair with carved swan supports extended
toward the terrace within one of the balanced pair
of newly added bay windows that augmented the
width of the living room. The whiteness of the
interior and the traditional desk and chair were
synergistically complementary to each other.

DINING ROOM (PREVIOUS PAGES)

Hodgins carried pale hues of blue and ivory in the living room into the dining room, which was situated across the entrance hall, on the opposite side of the apartment. He curtained the balanced pair of oversized bay windows in blue-and-ivory striped silk and upholstered the Rose Tarlow Chippendale-style dining chairs with ice-blue cut velvet. Their frames were finished in distressed white wood. The pale colors contrasted effectively with the patina of the mahogany dining table, buffet, and regency-style writing desk that was recessed into one of the bays.

An ivory carpet patterned in a high-low geometric design set off the hand-etched and crackle-finished dining table—its surface reflecting the natural light filtering into the room through one of the pair of bay windows.

STUDY

Mr. and Mrs. Weiner asked Hodgins for a wood-paneled study for "warmth." He specified pale maple paneling without much grain, maintaining calmness and simplicity in the room along with a color scheme of ivory, blue, and gray. The pleasant color scheme, with its minutely subtle differences in hue and texture, comprised a Steven King grid-patterned carpet handwoven in Tibet and upholstery materials including parchment chenille covering the sofa and gray-blue-and-white striped silk on the armchairs. The soft-blue tea silk curtains framed a compelling view of Boston and the hovering sky, which was further amplified by the projecting bay window.

MASTER-BEDROOM BAY

Stationary curtains of luxurious striped silk taffeta, and undercurtains of sheer white embroidered organdy, served as an elegant backdrop for a Louis XVI–style black lacquer bureau plat detailed in ormolu and the flanking pair of painted and gilded open-arm shield-back chairs. The yellow-and-white jacquard covering the chairs, with its small-scale pattern of blossoms, subtly accented the arrangement.

MASTER BEDROOM

Hodgins created the "happy, sunny, yellow master bedroom" that Mrs. Weiner wanted. He covered the floor in luxe specially colored pale-yellow-and-white linen carpet from Stark Carpet, patterned in damask, and curtained the pair of bay windows in alternating striped panels of ivory and yellow silk taffeta that were seamed together. He also dressed the bed in a buttercup-yellow silk taffeta coverlet, lightly quilted in large squares, adorned with small handmade rosettes and contrast-ruched in its seam on three sides. The additional infusion of white—the woven cotton and linen upholstered headboard and bedskirt, a silk bed pillow meticulously handsewn in seed pearls, and the built-in cabinetry and classic trim—amplified the cheerfulness of the suite.

MR. AND MRS. JULIAN COHEN

Boston, Massachusetts, 2004

In 2004, Julian and Carol Cohen purchased a condominium in the Back Bay neighborhood of Boston and hired Hodgins and Richard Sammons to completely redesign the sixteenth-floor apartment. Sammons had recently collaborated with Hodgins on Mr. and Mrs. Cohen's apartment in Palm Beach. Both commissions resulted in interiors that were understated and classically beautiful.

ENTRANCE ROTUNDA

Hodgins anchored the domed entrance rotunda in Mr. and Mrs. Cohen's apartment with a very fine regency rosewood rent table and a pair of Italian empire stools that were upholstered in pale-blue-and-beige silk brocade. The handsomely executed hall opened to the dining room and its boundless views of Back Bay, Cambridge, and the Charles River.

LIVING ROOM TOWARD FIREPLACE

The handsomely appointed marble-topped table displaying an imposing Degas bronze served as foreground for the Louis XVI limestone mantel and an oil portrait by Mary Cassatt. The classical detailing in the living room was augmented by built-in cabinetry and the extraordinary display of Chinese Export porcelain.

LIVING ROOM

The living room was furnished with a compilation of handsome antiques and underscored by a handmade Abadjian Romanian wool carpet. Its restrained shades of beige, soft blue, green, and saffron influenced the color palette for the room.

Hodgins arranged the living room with three sitting areas that radiated from an Italian neoclassical carved and giltwood center table. He upholstered a pair of sofas in beige chenille damask and accented them with pillows in lustrous silk taffetas and exquisite embroideries. Antique armchairs, including a pair of Scandinavian neoclassical parcel giltwood models, and exemplary French and Italian tables enhanced the groupings.

LIVING ROOM AT SETTEE

An antique hand-painted French settee luxuriously upholstered in blue cotton chenille and its accenting salmon brocade pillow contributed vibrancy to the living room, which drew additional color from the carpet. The mirrored ceiling beam heightened the interior and echoed Eugene Boudin's oil "La Baie de Douarnenez."

LIVING ROOM TOWARD PICTURE WINDOW

Hodgins deferred to the magnificence of the Boston Public Garden and outlying cityscape when decorating the living room. He specified muted colors and silken and crackle lacquered finishes that did not overpower the panoramic setting. The fine furnishings offsetting the sofa included a nineteenth-century empire bronze mounted mahogany and ebonized wood bouillotte table and a Chinese-style coffee table with allover classic phoenix decoration and gilded fillets.

DINING ROOM
TOWARD SERVER

The mahogany dining table, made by Joseph Gerte Company of Boston, was in harmony with the Sheraton-style sideboard, the pastel portrait by Mary Cassatt, and the distinctive display of rare eighteenth-century English creamware. The classically detailed elevation articulated the understatement of Hodgins's and Sammons's design.

DINING ROOM
(FOLLOWING PAGES)

Hodgins enriched the dining room with walls that were glazed soft yellow and framed its views of the city between stationary curtains of luxurious cream silk taffeta. He also refinished the shield-back dining chairs in slightly distressed old-world white, and upholstered them in celadon woven cotton. The mirrored cornice with its trellised overlay glamorized the interior.

LIBRARY TOWARD WINDOWS

Classically detailed pine paneling, a handmade Abadjian wool carpet, and a color scheme of shades of beige, blue, and cocoa endowed the library with warmth and comfort. Furniture sumptuously upholstered in chenille, damask, and woven herringbone cotton also warmed the interior and embodied Hodgins's belief that "upholstered pieces must not only be comfortable, they must look comfortable."

Hodgins placed an oversized chaise longue into a corner of the library, giving the room another mode of comfortable seating. He also introduced additional touches of color into the setting. The linen pillow on the chaise was striped in beige, green, and rose.

MASTER BEDROOM AT DESK

Architectural detailing evolving from an arrangement of built-in cabinets organized and separated an antique desk from the sleeping area of the bedroom. The diversity of the offsetting chairs and their respective upholstery—solid, specially colored blue leather and ivory-and-pale-blue zigzag-patterned cotton—complemented the setting.

MASTER BEDROOM

Hodgins brightened the classically paneled master bedroom with morning-glory chintz, setting the blue-and-green floral print against sky-blue carpet patterned in an ivory trellis. The refreshing, impressionist décor was also enhanced by subtle patterns and textures, including the blue-and-ivory woven cotton covering the Louis XVI–style bench placed at the foot of the bed.

PRIVATE RESIDENCE

Brookline, Massachusetts, 2004

In 1981, Hodgins's client and her husband commissioned him to decorate their classic New England vernacular house in Brookline, Massachusetts. It was sited on over ten acres of sylvan property. They wanted "a classic look with no color and no fancies" for the interiors of their new home and Hodgins "gave it to them." He used a color palette of off-white, pale cream, and camel, composing luxurious, subtly textured materials, carpets, and lacquered finishes. The noncolors created understated, "clean-line" interiors, allowing the focus—through expansive walls of glass—on the outside where Hodgins's clients developed the grounds with extensive gardens and added koi fish to a large pond on the property.

In 2004, Hodgins's client purchased "raw space" on the top floor of a new condominium building not far from her house. The spacious plan, which was originally conceived as a four-bedroom apartment, was reconfigured masterfully with a large master bedroom suite and guest bedroom by architects John MacDonald, principal of Morehouse Mac-Donald & Associates, and Vu Alexander, associate architect. Together, they laid out the entire apartment and added to every room in the tall-ceilinged interior "as much glass with sliders [as the client] could get," re-creating the generous exposure to the outdoors she had at her previous house.

Hodgins did all the interior detailing of the apartment. He added tall baseboards, door casings, and crown moldings, and burnished with gold leaf the trim running below the living room moldings "to create a little sparkle and direct the eye upwards." Most important, "he helped his client move from her house, used everything from there and [oversaw] it all in his fine, caring and gentlemanly manner."

LIVING ROOM CLOSEUP

Hodgins juxtaposed a pair of handsome eighteenth-century Swedish barrel-back armchairs with a Chinese-style coffee table covered in fine linen and lacquered creamy ivory. He and his clients found the chairs on a shopping trip to New York during the early 1980s. They were in terrible condition. Their legs "splayed out" and their upholstery "popped." Undaunted by the poor state of the antique chairs, Hodgins knew that they could be restored and contribute singularly to the living room.

LIVING ROOM ENTRANCE

MacDonald and Alexander placed the living room on axis with the entrance gallery of the apartment. Limestone tile paving the gallery floor continued into the living room and maintained unity of the two interiors, which were further enhanced by the heightened baseboard and tall entranceway.

LIVING ROOM OVERVIEW (FOLLOWING PAGES)

Hodgins furnished the living room, which spanned the entire width of the apartment, with two principal sitting areas, setting them on opposite sides of the fireplace. The limestone mantel is especially handsome. It was made by Chesney's of London and is similar to the chimneypiece designed by the influential English architect Sir John Soane for his own drawing room. The antique mahogany men's dressing table flanking the mantel is Louis XVI.

Hodgins arranged one of the sitting areas against the backdrop of an expansive wall of glass, maximizing the openness and exposure to natural light so valued by his client. The colorless and luxurious upholstery materials— silk, moiré, and damask—and the creamy ivory lacquered, gilded, and pale dove-gray finishes of the coffee table and pair of chairs compose a setting of restrained elegance.

LIVING ROOM AT PAINTING

Hodgins anchored the sitting area at the front of the living room with a rolled-arm sofa of the same design and upholstered as its counterpart. He covered the flanking oversized Italian regency-style armchairs in antique white damask and finished the Chinese curved coffee table in ivory lacquer, contributing subtle variations between the two seating arrangements. The antique black painted table with gilded details and round chinoiserie side table placed alongside the sliding glass door individualized the grouping.

LIVING ROOM AT PAINTING CLOSEUP

Hodgins's "exacting placement" of the furniture from his client's house made her feel immediately at home in her new apartment. He knew precisely where everything should go, including the client's art and accessories, which she says, "give her rooms color." The design of alternating squares in the white wool carpet and the linear detailing of the entranceway casing complemented the "classicism and modernity" of the fireplace mantel.

DINING ROOM TOWARD SERVER

Hodgins infused the dining room with simplicity and refinement. He detailed the room with wainscoting and crown molding that was restrained and surrounded the dining table with handsomely carved Louis XVI–style Cole Porter arm and side chairs made by Frederick P. Victoria. The wool carpet was specially colored in graduated shades of beige.

DINING ROOM TOWARD WINDOW

Stronger neutral tones than the pale palette in the living room comprised the dining room. The Karl Springer oval dining table was specially made in ivory goatskin parchment and highly lacquered, the dining chairs were upholstered in bisque leather and dove-gray cotton taffeta on their outside backs, and the curtains were made of taupe silk canvas. The client's accessories, including a collection of chinoiserie hat boxes that she and her husband found in China, and a variety of orchid plants that she lovingly cultivates, personalize the room.

LIBRARY CLOSEUP

Built-in bookcases filled with handsomely bound series of books and accessories from China serve as backdrop for an Italian Louis XVI walnut bureau plat, a Louis XV carved beechwood fauteuil, and an eighteenth-century English side chair. The large red ware ginger jar displayed underneath the desk is one of the countless accessories Hodgins's client "shopped for" in the walk-in "secret closet" she "visited regularly" behind the receptionist's desk at Hodgins's office. It was always stocked with shelves of wonderful "finds" from Hodgins's travels. The coral-colored linen tape binding the bamboo sisal carpet contrasts with the neutral décor.

LIBRARY

Hodgins decorated the library in a monochromatic color palette of camel and complemented it with Cowtan & Tout paisley silk patterned in restrained shades of rose and soft blue on a pale camel ground. He upholstered a split-back chair in the paisley and used it for a pair of sofa pillows.

PRIVATE RESIDENCE

Washington, D.C., 2008

The client's penthouse duplex in Washington is the second apartment Hodgins decorated for her there. She purchased the apartment for a quick getaway and to give her college-age daughter another place to nest during school breaks, summer vacations, and whenever the urge strikes. The apartment was planned as a pied-à-terre.

Hodgins and his client "are both extreme perfectionists and it seems that they were both eager to be more audacious in the concept and aesthetic choices" with the apartment as it was "not thought to be a permanent residence." The interiors were "geared" more so to the client's daughter, the modern architecture of the building, and to be "more experimental" than her previous commissions with Hodgins.

The apartment was also "Modern" as only William Hodgins would create it. Although he "is from a different generation, he still embraces all design with his masterful eye and puts it all together" with the "same elements of taste and quality" and his own aesthetic, which is always fresh, classic, and perfectly edited.

ENTRANCE HALL

A console table finished in faux parchment and the classically framed and brightly gilded round mirror anchoring the entrance hall were indicators of impeccable style of the apartment. The imposing portrait of a pack of leopards reflected in the mirror previewed the collection of majestic black-and-white photographs of animals in the African wilderness taken by Nick Brandt and displayed throughout the apartment. The blanc de Chine lamp is by Christopher Spitzmiller.

CLOSEUP OF SOFA

Pillows covered in ice-blue silk canvas and lilac silk taffeta contrasted subtly with the chenille upholstery of the sofa and the complementing chenille pillows. The tender colors softened the interiors and confer simplicity and translucency as does the clear acrylic coffee table that the client says "catches light."

LIVING ROOM WRITING DESK

A magnificent contemporary writing desk designed by
Vicente Wolf placed at the far end of the living room
augmented the mesmerizing interior and reflected light,
shapes, and fragments of color from its sleek white lacquer
top and pair of mirrored and polished stainless steel legs.
The architecturally inspired legs, particularly striking, reflect
elements of the pair of Louis XVI–style chairs finished
in old-world white and upholstered in lavender silk.

LIVING ROOM

Spare accents of pastel shades offset a backdrop of "perfect
white-white" painstakingly formulated for the living room
floor and walls and ceilings throughout the apartment
by Marcus Pluntke, creating ethereal and awe-inspiring
magnificence, especially in the living room. Here, various
textures, including "bleach-white" chenille made by Leni's
Inc., covered a capacious L-shaped sofa and chaise longue
luxuriously skirted in ivory bullion fringe. The white
cotton sheers screening the walls of glass and an outsized
carpet composed of innumerable eighteen-inch squares of
white hides that were sewn together represented Hodgins's
distinctive and timeless approach to modern design.

The restrained pattern and texture of the hide carpet
underscored the comfortably designed and luxuriously
appointed chaise longue placed in a windowed corner of the
living room, alongside the fireplace. The tranquil grouping,
which was offset by a white metal zigzag table and an early
twentieth-century Venetian mirrored gueridon, articulated
the "relationship of shape to shape, weights and textures"
and serenely infused light—all essences of Hodgins's design genius.

DINING BANQUETTE

Hodgins set a timeless Eero Saarinen white tulip table from Knoll against an armless dining banquette covered in an enchanting blue-and-ivory Indian floral canvas print. The pair of Louis XVI–style oval-back side chairs finished in old-world white and upholstered in soft blue leather, with contrasting gingham backs, confirmed that classic designs, regardless of the period, are always compatible.

DAUGHTER'S DEN

Although the apartment was designed and decorated with the client's daughter clearly in mind, the plan included a den specifically for her use, a cozy and self-contained lounge separated from the connecting living room by a tall floor-to-ceiling frosted glass door.

Pastel shades reminiscent of the living room maintained consistency of design in the den. A textural carpet boldly striped in seven colors, including rose, aqua, pale green, and chocolate brown, introduced pattern to the décor and synchronized with the array of vibrant pillows casually arranged on the oyster-colored L-shaped leather sofa.

Unusual furniture contributed character to the den. The John Saladino coffee table with its Crema Marfel stone tray top was supported by a cold-steel base resting innovatively on three curved legs; the James Duncan sculptural Botero stool placed alongside the sofa was lacquered in glossy pale lavender.

DEN

A commodious arrangement of
built-in cabinetry painted white
was the principal backdrop in the
den. In this combined library/
sitting room located on the
second floor of the apartment,
soft blue Travers cotton covered
the capacious sofa, ottoman, and
split-back upholstered chair, and
conferred senses of comfort and
restfulness inherent in Hodgins's
decorating. Additional allure
came from the Peter Fasano white
silk pillows specially painted
with large blue square dots and
the late 1970s French coffee
table with gilded metal frame,
chamfered corners, and crackled
linen painted top that Lucien
Allaire and Karen Hess, Hodgins's
longstanding and highly valued
office manager, purchased long
distance, by telephone, when
it was auctioned in Paris.

MASTER BEDROOM

Hodgins infused delicate shades of blue against a refreshing palette of white in the master bedroom. He curtained the expansive windowed wall in sky-blue silk taffeta with an exacting ripplefold heading and covered the floor in a vanilla ground carpet contrastingly patterned in a soft blue octagonal trellis. The contemporary-style bench placed at the foot of the bed and upholstered in square biscuit tufted chenille—also in soft blue—broadened the tableau of "femininity expressed in a very simple way."

In a corner of the bedroom, Hodgins placed an upholstered highback armchair against the luxe backdrop of sky-blue silk taffeta and the smartly patterned carpet. The genteel chair, with its elegant stature, was particularly appealing. Its regal silhouette was flattered by white cotton matelasse and a scallop-edged skirt that curtseyed gracefully to the floor.

DAUGHTER'S BEDROOM

The daughter's bedroom was "genius and done only as William Hodgins would do." She selected its dynamic colors. Deep aquamarine paint, glazed and overglazed by Marcus Pluntke to achieve a high-gloss patina, covered the floor. The window curtains were fabricated in chartreuse silk taffeta.

Sequins randomly adorning the sheer undercurtains and silver dots specially painted by Peter Fasano on the cotton coverlet and pillows were also dazzling. The pureness of the materials melded with the clarity of the white leather covering the huge Italian bed and very modern chair.

DAUGHTER'S BEDROOM CLOSEUP

The case goods in the bedroom were custom-made. They included a pair of simply designed five-drawer chests that were lacquered white "like a Kahr" as the Boston-area cabinet maker pronounced in his native tongue and "labeled the finish sample that [was] finally selected." The cabinetry and the composition of the bedroom were complemented by Christopher Spitzmiller's pair of lamps—specially colored and glazed in a scrumptious shade of red.

MRS. AUDREY WINTMAN

Boston, Massachusetts, 2009

Audrey Wintman and her husband Melvin Wintman originally hired Hodgins to decorate their house in suburban Boston during the early 1980s. Later, Hodgins decorated their oceanfront apartment in Palm Beach, Florida.

This assignment for Mrs. Wintman was the decoration of her condominium in a new building that was being built in the Back Bay neighborhood of Boston. The three-bedroom apartment, with its sweeping views of the city, was an ideal aerie. Mrs. Wintman, who had always wanted to feel like she was living in a New York penthouse, achieved her wish through Hodgins's thoughtfully decorated interiors and the meticulous architectural work of David Ferris, senior designer at the Boston firm CBT/Childs Bertman Tseckares.

LIVING ROOM FIREPLACE CLOSEUP

Accessories symmetrically arranged by the fireplace complemented the eclectic compilation of furniture composed of French, Swedish, and English styles. The accessories in themselves were notable. They included the gilded bronze leaf-back wall lights, the peony-filled ceramic cachepots, and the small Christopher Spitzmiller blanc de Chine lamps.

ENTRANCE HALL TOWARD LIVING ROOM

White limestone tile paving the entrance hall of the apartment introduced the airiness of the interiors and underscored a pair of identically scaled upholstered banquettes. The banquettes, which Hodgins designed with biscuit tufted seats, were covered in the "palest" toast silk velvet and copiously skirted in bullion fringe. Silk pillows, meticulously brocaded in a spare floral pattern, alluded to the soft, calming palette in the adjoining living room.

Hodgins furnished the living room with two seating areas. He placed one grouping alongside the fireplace, anchoring the arrangement with an oversized settee upholstered in cream damask. The Agra carpet, the brown Shantung silk pillows, and the Swedish chair—with its luxe-cut peach silk velvet upholstery—subtly infused color into the setting.

LIVING ROOM

Hodgins arranged the principal seating area in the living room against the backdrop of full-length windows overlooking the Boston cityscape. He framed the windows with curtains of creamy silk taffeta, softening the overpowering views and integrating them with the natural and diaphanous qualities of the interior.

Traditional furniture, finished in mahogany, also complemented the interior. Hodgins likes "strong" and dark wood pieces in his rooms. He places "that type of furniture next to white, and the white becomes weightier." The bouillotte table standing alongside the sofa was particularly handsome. It enlivened everything around it, including the French coffee table that was lacquered in blanc de Chine.

LIBRARY

Rich shades of chocolate brown and creamy beige composed the library, creating an interior of great warmth and comfort. The principal influence in the room was the carpet. Its dynamic design in a two-toned geometric pattern offset furniture upholstered in soft brown leather and beige and cream cottons. English-style tables finished in dark walnut and high-gloss mahogany and built-in bookcases, thoughtfully accessorized, augmented the interior.

LIBRARY VIEW
INTO LIVING ROOM

A split-back upholstered chair, coupled with an English-style tray table, conveyed the importance of comfort and practicality in Hodgins's interiors. The end table lamp and the small lamp arranged on the bookcase shelf also expressed his ardent attention to lighting. The double doorway behind the chair frames a view of the adjoining living room, revealing its Louis XVI–style mahogany card table and oval-back armchairs that Hodgins upholstered in exquisite peach strié damask.

DINING ROOM CLOSEUP

Dark wood furniture also balanced the tableau in the dining room. Hodgins designed the walnut server, detailing it with mirrored panels and doors that have elliptical mullions. The reflective surfaces enlivened the room and proffered a glimpse of the beige Tibetan carpet and its subtle, allover pattern of dots.

DINING ROOM

Hodgins set Mrs. Wintman's favored color of soft peach against a restful background of beige in the dining room of her apartment. He dressed the only window in the room with stationary curtains, creating them from alternating stripes of soft peach and creamy silk taffetas that were seamed together. Hodgins also upholstered the Louis VXI–style dining chairs in specially colored peach leather, and, for contrast, covered their outside backs in beige-and-white cotton check. The chairs were handsome accompaniments to the mahogany dining table.

MRS. HELAINE ALLEN

Boston, Massachusetts, 2010

When Helaine Allen hired Hodgins to decorate her new apartment in Boston, he had already completed—over a period of forty years—five homes for her and her late husband Alvin Allen. Mrs. Allen was simplifying her life. She sold the family house in Chestnut Hill, Massachusetts, which Hodgins had decorated traditionally, and moved in town. The present assignment resulted in an apartment that was casual and less formal than Mrs. Allen's former home.

LIVING ROOM CLOSEUP

Hodgins outfitted the living room with a French lacquered coffee table—one of his favorite models—and a French provincial commode, both from Mrs. Allen's former home. Helaine Allen admires Hodgins's ability to "use everything" he can from a client's home, including furniture he finds stored in the attic or basement.

DINING AREA

Hodgins incorporated a built-in banquette and dining table into his plan for the living room. He upholstered the seating as well in textured parchment linen and highlighted it with a succession of solid silk and hand-painted linen and silk pillows in colors of soft blue, citrus yellow, and pale pink.

The extendable dining table had a lustrous parchment-colored finish and its classic details included a fluted columnar pedestal. A pair of regency-style armchairs adorned with gilded lions' head terminals and paw feet completed the seating.

LIVING ROOM (FOLLOWING PAGES)

Refreshing pastels, graphically bold carpet woven in an allover pattern of large ivory stars on a beige ground, and generous views of the Boston Public Garden distinguished Mrs. Allen's living room, which Hodgins arranged without "crowding" the floor plan. He placed a large sofa covered in textured parchment linen against the principal wall and balanced it with a pair of split-back chairs upholstered in pale-blue twill. Dazzling colors emanated from Peter Fasano's painted cotton and silk pillows on the sofa and the striped silk cloth draping the round end table.

LIVING ROOM AT FIREPLACE

A copiously fringed ottoman upholstered in button-tufted, textured parchment linen anchored additional seating arranged alongside the living room fireplace. A third split-back upholstered chair, which was also covered in pale-blue twill, maintained the consistency of pastel colors permeating the living room.

STUDY

Hodgins deviated from pastel colors when he decorated the study. He opted for medium hunter-green walls and white paneled wainscoting that contrasted effectively with the engaging Clarence House printed linen he specified for the curtains, sofa pillows, and chair seat. Fervent shades of tomato, green, tan, and cocoa "depicting a playful and fanciful design of gibbons, birds and flora in an exotic sub-tropic fantasy" radiated from a beige-colored ground and complemented the natural hues of the sofa upholstery and carpet. The green nubuck suede covering the Louis XVI–style armchair introduced additional color to the study.

STUDY CLOSEUP

Hodgins placed a Hepplewhite-style armchair against a backdrop of natural textures and finishes. The beige tweed material covering the sofa, the parchment glaze of the parsons-style end table, and the bamboo wool sisal carpet with green binding all contributed character to the setting without imposing on the handsome printed linen covering the chair seat and pillows resting against the arms of the sofa.

GAME TABLE AT WINDOW

A Louis XVI–style mahogany game table handsomely detailed with polished brass fittings created a hospitable venue for spirited rounds of bridge. The oval-back side chairs, with their old-world-white frames, beige textured leather upholstery, and contrasting beige-and-off-white cotton check on their outside backs, contributed stylishly to the arrangement.

CARD ROOM

Hodgins specified a monochromatic palette for the card room. He painted the walls kraft-bag brown and covered the floor with off-white carpet contrastingly patterned in a taupe octagonal trellis that reverberated stylishly with the beige-and-brown English printed linen covering the sofa and composing the window curtains. The French blue painted tops and lower shelves of the two-tiered brass end tables and the slate-blue textured linen pillows on the sofa display Hodgins's keen sense of color. The complementary but inexactly matched shades of blue finalized the interior.

MASTER BEDROOM

Helaine Allen has always had a "very difficult" time selecting material for her bedroom. When Hodgins was decorating the house in Chestnut Hill, she routinely "pasted [material samples] on the bedroom wall, laid on the floor," and looked up at the potential material, trying to make a decision. When Mrs. Allen couldn't choose, Hodgins "became annoyed" and told her to "select something!" However, it wasn't until Hodgins showed Mrs. Allen the guest bedroom in his Clarendon Street townhouse, with its classic, lushly patterned and beautifully shaded geranium chintz that she said, "That's it!" In fact, Mrs. Allen loved the Clarence House chintz so much that, even after living with the material for over thirty years, she asked Hodgins to repeat it in the present bedroom. He told her, "No, that's enough!" Fortunately, Hodgins showed Mrs. Allen a delightfully patterned off-white Cowtan & Tout textured linen print decorated with bouquets of hollyhocks in shades of blue, mauve, green, and brown that were connected by a flowing ribbon motif and interspersed obscurely with tiny golden-yellow butterflies. The material harmonized flawlessly with the ivory wool carpet, handwoven by Avena Carpets in diagonally patterned, double-shadowed quatrefoils in three soft shades of green, each one highlighted centrally with a tiny dot in light mauve pink.

8 "Mr. Hodgins". Interview with Gregory Richardson, December 7, 2010.

8 "spending a lot of time finding out what they like". Interview with William Hodgins, September 21, 2010.

8 "their feelings for their homes". Francis Levy, "Spontaneity and Surprise: Orchestrating Art and Antiques in a Manhattan Duplex," *Architectural Digest*, XL:5 (1983), 121.

8 "extraordinarily luxurious as they can be in a quiet, understated way". *Boston Globe*, October 5, 2000, Sec. H, p. 5.

8 reminiscent of Merchant-Ivory imprints. Interview with Gregory Richardson, December 8, 2010.

8 "reflect the quality of life and light in a room." Elaine Brooks, "Questions of Interior Design: The Answers from William Hodgins," *The World & I*, I:4 (1986), 478.

8 "glow behind the art and furniture". Lisa Cregan, "Comfort Really Lasts: A Classic Touch to a Virginia Home from Designer William Hodgins," *House Beautiful*, CXXXIII:1 (2008), 41.

10 "when he always had a pencil and paper in front of him." He had "control of his hand by the first grade". Interview with Patricia Barré, October 10, 2010.

10 "devoted to whatever he did and gave it his full attention". Ibid., August 13, 2011.

10 "big grand house". Interview with William Hodgins, September 14, 2010.

10 "ironmongery". Interview with William Hodgins, November 12, 2010.

10 "a short little gal wearing a toque like Queen Mary". Interview with William Hodgins, January 31, 2012.

10 "do something more suitable". Interview with William Hodgins, November 12, 2010.

10 "gopher". Ibid.

10 "barely get into [the room]". Interview with William Hodgins, September 14, 2010.

10 "nothing". Ibid.

10 "how lucky they were to have a job". Ibid.

10 "It drove his mother crazy". Christine Pittel, *House Beautiful-Great Style* (New York: Hearst Books, 1996), 38.

10 "always liked making things look better and appealing". Interview with William Hodgins, November 12, 2012.

10 "fascination". George Whitmore, "Design Dialogue: William Hodgins: A Little Romance in Boston," *Architectural Digest*, XLII:11 (1985), 98.

10–11 "came to the conclusion that you spend half of your conscious life at work so you better like it". Stacy Kunstel, "Interview-William Hodgins," *New England Home*, 11:4 (2007), 60.

11 "flamboyant and exotic". *Boston Globe*, op. cit.

11 "an interview of sorts" and "told him to come in the next day". Interview with William Hodgins, September 14, 2010.

11 "gopher". Ibid.

11 "liked young men". *Boston Globe*, op. cit.

11 "tag along for lunch once in awhile because he was tall, and spoke good English". Ibid.

11 "loved her shop". Ibid.

11 "proud and pleased". Interview with William Hodgins, September 14, 2010.

11 "she didn't understand why he would leave a good job to attend Parsons". Ibid.

11 "junior-junior assistant". Ibid.

11 "how to make estimates and do curtain treatments". Louis Postel and Andrea Brox, "William Hodgins NOW," *Design Times*, March/April, 1990, 36.

12 "unqualified recommendation". Application for Membership; *American Institute of Interior Designers*, July 15, 1964.

12 "quintessential". Brooks, op. cit., p. 471.

12 "pushed". Interview with William Hodgins, September 14, 2010.

12 "by chance". Ibid.

12 "paid close attention to Stanley". Ibid.

12 "quietly dazzling". Ibid.

12 "had never seen anything like Hadley's living room". Ibid.

12 "very simple". Ibid.

12 "of a beautiful [soft] quality". Ibid.

12 "seams that you could see". Ibid.

12 "You're hired". Ibid.

12 "teachers, respected friends, and cohorts". Apple Parish Bartlett & Susan Bartlett Crater, *Sister: The Life of Legendary American Interior Decorator Mrs. Henry Parish II* (New York: St. Martin's Press, 2000), p. 350.

12 "everything—scale, color, integrity". Whitmore, op. cit., p. 103.

12 "a room must be usable first, then it will always be inviting". Cregan, op. cit.

12 "They cared deeply". Kunstel, op. cit.

12 "too city, too big, too large, too everything". Interview with William Hodgins, September 21, 2010.

12 "sleepy university town". Florence de Dampierre, *The Decorator* (New York: Rizzoli, 1989), p. 105.

12 "wonderful size". Ibid.

12 "a very good bartender and an equally good waiter". Interview with William Hodgins, September 14, 2010.

13 "the young man who just came from New York". Interview with Helaine Allen, September 23, 2010.

13 "he would put her typewriter under the desk". Kunstel, op. cit., p. 62.

13 "working on an apartment for them was one of my first jobs when I moved to Boston. I had just started out on my own, I had virtually no clients, and I was referred by [Ben Cook] to work on one of their bedrooms because the job was too small for him". Jeffrey Simpson, "Classical Grace in Palm Beach," *Architectural Digest*, XLVII:11 (1990), 89.

13 "seized upon this classic American decorator who trained in New York". Interview with Gregory Richardson, September 21, 2010.

13 "wonderfully supportive encouragement". Interview with William Hodgins, October 10, 2010.

14 "all kinds of dilapidated shops in New York". Richard Fitzgerald, "When The 20th Century Moves In: Gloomy Victorian Lights Up," *House Beautiful*, CXIII:1 (1971), 54.

14 "where he gave them what they wanted—with taste!" Interview with Gitty Scheft, September 11, 2010.

14 "strict taskmaster". Interview with William Hodgins, September 14, 2010.

14 "a quiet retreat, lined and upholstered in Swiss linen—highlighted with soft silk and madras, a background for a very personal collection of furniture and objects". The Jr. League of Boston, Inc.: First Decorators' Show House in Massachusetts, p. 28.

14 "large, crisp, and soft with carpets and ribbons". Ibid., p. 29.

14 "hooked on Hodgins". Interview with Carol Feinberg Cohen, August 21, 2010.

14 "serene colors". Ann Faraday, "How to Make Your Dreams Work for You," *House & Garden*, CXLI:3 (1972), 85.

14 "insight into your sleeping life". Ibid.

14 "serene dreams". Ibid.

15 "comfortable modern furniture, romantic antiques, and modern art." The Jr. League of Boston, Inc.: Decorators' Show House 1972, p. 11.

15 "sweet chocolate". Mary Jane Pool et al. "Introducing 6 New H & G Colors," *House & Garden*, CXLII:9 (1972), 84.

15 "shell". Ibid., p. 85.

15 "marvelously versatile". Ibid., p. 84.

16 "Hodgins magically transformed". Interview with Joan Daniels, September 26, 2010.

17 "found Bill". Interview with Sophie Engelhard, October 5, 2010.

17 "why more interior designers and architects don't come to our attention in Boston; it is a city with so much inherent taste and character". Paige Rense, "People Are the Issue," *Architectural Digest*, XXXVIII:1 (1981), 10.

17 "pleased to be showing the work of William Hodgins". Ibid.

17 "New England Charm". Valentine Lawford, "New England Charm," *Architectural Digest*, XXXVIII:1 (1981), 52.

17 "aim was to create a personal ambience: romantic, but lightly so". Ibid., pp. 55–56.

17 "old-world decorations". Fact & Credit Sheets, January 23, 1980, Courtesy of *Architectural Digest* and Condé Nast archives.

17 "a light-hearted mood". Lawford, op. cit., p. 57.

18 "special". Fact & Credit Sheets, January 23, 1980, Courtesy of *Architectural Digest* and Condé Nast archives.

18 "Paige Rense telegrammed Hodgins". Western Union Mailgram, April 8, 1981, Courtesy of William Hodgins Incorporated.

18 "wanted a bright atmosphere". Paige Rense, "People Are the Issue," *Architectural Digest*, XXXVIII:9 (1981), 20.

18 "a contemporary feeling to a design that [fit] a delightfully old-fashioned way of living". Ibid.

18 "period". Ibid.

18 "stiffly formal". Ibid.

18 "palest mauve". Fact & Credit Sheets, September 26, 1980, Courtesy of *Architectural Digest* and Condé Nast archives.

18 "visionary husband-and-wife textile designers". Courtesy of PRWeb.

19 "odd, slightly off-center peaked turret and weathered shingles". Carol Vogel, "Mistaken Identity," *The New York Times Magazine*, August 23, 1987, 36.

19 "one of those whimsical English garden structures known as follies, mysteriously washed up on the Massachusetts shore". Ibid.

23 "never been so taken with a place". Elaine Greene, "Old World White," *House & Garden*, CLIX:1 (1987), 97.

23 "an infinity of colors between chalk and stone". Ibid., p. 94.

23 "focus on forms". Loredana Mascheroni, "Il fascino discreto del classic," *SPAZIOCASA*, 9 (1995), 8.

23 "in a white room there is no place to hide". Elizabeth H. Hunter, "William Hodgins in the City . . . And in the Country," *House Beautiful*, CXXXIII: 10 (1991), 79.

23 "old-world white". Greene, op. cit.

23 "shorthand not only for creamy, soft, old-looking color". Ibid.

23 "a state of mind". Ibid.

23 "very subtle textured surface". Vogel, op. cit., p. 38.

23 "from looking too pristine, too antiseptic". Ibid., p. 40.

23 "The Quiet Charm of Classic". Mascheroni, op. cit., p. 7.

23 "the master of the pale, neutral palette". Ibid.

23 "unbelievably shabby and depressing—brightly colored, the foyer dotted with crystal chandeliers, the whole thing lacking coherence". Francesca Stanfill, "Passion Makes Perfect," *Vogue*, CLXXVI:11 (1986), 426.

26 "He ripped out tons of unattractive marble and replaced it with much softer, more elegant stone. He then added mullions, baseboards, cornices, wainscoting, French doors, fireplaces and wood floors to all three of its floors. He also enhanced the front of the house with a new foyer that had stylish high round win-

dows and turned the [unfortunate] looking basement into a [handsome] theatre, billiards room, wine cellar, and exercise suite". e-mail from Linda Taubman, January 8, 2011.

26 "he [has always spent] an occasional Monday through Wednesday, scouting for pieces he thinks will appeal to his clients, and then takes them to see his pre-selections on Thursday". Susan Sheehan, "Lighter Shades of Pale," *Architectural Digest*, LXIII:1 (2006), 140.

26 "ran the gamut, from Mallett on New Bond Street to Portobello Road". Interview with Linda Taubman, September 13, 2010.

27 "think carefully about each piece of furniture". Interview with Laura Munder, September 21, 2010.

28 "how it could be used". Ibid.

28 "they want to live". Interview with Linda Taubman, September 13, 2010.

28 "a different way of life". Interview with Laura Munder, September 21, 2010.

28 "never condescending". Ibid.

28 "feel comfortable. That's part of who he is". Ibid.

28 "serenity". Stanfill, op. cit., p. 425.

28 "a variation on white". Ibid., p. 423.

28 "fancy," "fussy," nor "stuffy". Interview with Linda Taubman, September 13, 2010.

28 "disparate styles and periods". Stanfill, op. cit., p. 425.

30 "calm". Ibid., p. 421.

30 "particular weakness". Ibid., p. 426.

30 "all which taught Hodgins a lot". Interview with William Hodgins, January 31, 2012.

30 "Slightly offbeat, unusual chairs can add a lot of [style] to a room without furnishing it too much". Stanfill, op. cit., p. 426.

30 "to honor outstanding designers working in the field". Interview with Lester Dundes, December, 1985.

30 "generous outreach". Interview with Patricia Black, September 27, 2010.

30 "very early efforts". Interview with Robert Sinclair, November 3, 2010.

30 "the two hit the telephones". Judith Davidsen, "AIDS Hospice," *Interior Design*, LXI:3 (1990), 204.

30 "colors must be upbeat, but soft, the design not complicate hospice work, create additional chores". Ibid.

30 "down to the depths of institutional atmospheres". Ibid.

31 "dressed up". Interview with Charles Spada, November 20, 2010.

31 "keep their doors shut". Ibid.

31 "a better quality of life for the people who would be using the space". Ed Mueller, "Designing from the HEART," *Design Times*, March/April 1990, 41.

32 "unparalleled". Paige Rense, *Architectural Digest* 100, XLVII:9 (1990), 2.

32 "photographic examples of the designers' work, descriptions of their design principles

and procedures, and practical data concerning their staffs and fee structures". Ibid.

32 "a true maestro of impressionistic color and light". Karol DeWulf Nickell, "From the Editor," *Traditional Home*, VII:11 (1995), 4.

32 "had set their sights on him prior to breaking ground". Pamela J. Wilson, "Artful Elegance," *Traditional Home*, VII:11 (1995), 89.

32 "didn't begin the job until he learned as much as he could about Mr. and Mrs. Bernon and their visions for the house". Ibid., p. 90.

32 "who they are, what they are and how they want to live". Interview with Joan Daniels, September 26, 2010.

32 "is one hundred percent for his clients". Interview with Jimmy Congema, November 11, 2010.

32 "wants the best for them". Interview with Jim Woolems, November 10, 2010.

32 "present people with total schemes". Whitmore, op. cit., p. 92.

32 "to pick and choose from up to one hundred and fifty samples and discuss them in terms of texture, pattern and color. Hodgins gets to know his clients this way, since he says, as long as it isn't attached to their sofa or chair or [curtains], clients can express themselves freely. It's not threatening [to them] ". Ibid.

32 "insists that both husband and wife participate in the decision making and that they spend at least a day with him reviewing concepts and prospective purchases". Ibid.

34 "minimalist, but not stark". Wilson, op. cit., p. 90.

34 "in this pared-down setting". Ibid., p. 97.

34 "it would stand out like a jewel". Ibid.

35 "full house". Interview with Penny Matteson, February 4, 2011.

35 "Blue Denim". e-mail from Lucien Allaire, February 23, 2011.

35 "extravagant bouquets of roses in multi shades of blue on an off-white linen ground". Ibid.

35 "massive". Judith Thurman, "Americans in Paris," *Architectural Digest*, LV:11 (1998), 227.

35 "flew to Paris on Mr. and Mrs. Rohatyn's behalf [to] get a feeling for the rooms and their light". Ibid., pp. 229–230.

35 "utterly gracious about facilitating the transition, [sent Hodgins] the floor plans and swatches of the paint, carpeting and [curtains]". Ibid., p. 231.

35 "a comfortable private home within a large public residence". Ibid., p. 229.

35 "private floor to be cozy and beckoning". Ibid.

35 "with a feeling of American informality". Ibid.

35 "conducive to quiet suppers, intimate teas, family visits and weekends of reading". Ibid.

35 "a color scheme that was warmer and more European than the one at their New York home". Ibid., p. 231.

36 "an American [variation] on English country, with printed materials used discreetly and antiques mixed with comfortably streamlined sofas and chairs". Ibid.

36 "a cache of desks, commodes, armoires and tables". Ibid., p. 232.

36 "resisted the impulse to overstuff". Ibid.

36 "flatter the shapely windows and lovely garden views". Ibid.

36 "encouraged by the intimacy of the space". Ibid.

36 "tactile [materials] and soft colors". Ibid.

36 "generous, big and full bouquets of roses in soft-to-brilliant shades of corals, pinks and crimson with stems, leaves and vines in soothing celadon green". e-mail from Lucien Allaire, February 23, 2011.

36 "gave the bedroom atmosphere". Thurman, op. cit., p. 232.

36 "high-speed course". Ibid.

36 "start to finish". Ibid.

36 "flawlessly—no mistakes". e-mail from Lucien Allaire, February 5, 2011.

36 "shipped from Boston to Miami to France and arrived unbroken". Ibid.

36 "the artisans and the installers. [They] were gratified and a little surprised when their hostess made a thank-you speech in fluent French". Thurman, op. cit.

36 "recognized an ASID professional interior designer who has made outstanding contributions toward achieving design excellence. The award is based on the winner's professional achievements, as exemplified by his or her work, which must demonstrate creative and innovative concepts that have advanced the profession of interior design". ASID, Icon, Fall 2001, 37.

37 "a special pull-out poster highlighting the genealogy of American interior designers". Newell Turner, "Editorial," House Beautiful, CLIII:4 (2011), 63.

37 "Family Tree" of "trailblazing" interior designers "who have wowed us with their style". Newell Turner et al. "House Beautiful: American Design," House Beautiful, CLIII:4 (2011).

37 "Grand Masters of Design who have defined American style". Michael Boodro et al. "Grand Masters of Design," Elle Décor, CLXXVI (2011), 136, and CLXXXVI (2012), 100.

38 "relaxed feel". Fact & Credit Sheets, October 28, 1982, Courtesy of Architectural Digest and Condé Nast archives.

38 "informal" and "spontaneous". Francis Levy, "Spontaneity and Surprise," Architectural Digest, XL:5 (1983), 121.

43 "tone" and "texture". Ibid.

43 "a nice surprise". Interview with Elizabeth Rohatyn, July 24, 2010.

44 "guest-house-turned-home". Anne Coffin, "Down East Sophistication," Architectural Digest, XLI:8 (1984), 119.

44 "coastal forest and farmland". Ibid.

44 "Masterpieces!" Interview with Millicent Monks, August 25, 2010.

44 "casually landscaped". Fact & Credit Sheets, December 30, 1982, Courtesy of Architectural Digest and Condé Nast archives.

44 "could enjoy for twelve months of the year". Coffin, op. cit., p. 119.

46 "open and inviting". Fact & Credit Sheets,

December 30, 1982, Courtesy of Architectural Digest and Condé Nast archives.

46 "the rooms [in the house] were intended for entertaining". Coffin, op. cit., p. 120.

48 "a home of intriguing dualities: part urban, part suburban; part contemporary, part traditional". Carol Vogel, "Combining the Old with the New," Architectural Digest, XXXIX:9 (1982), 179.

48 "a character of its own". Ibid.

50 "synchronize with the period pieces". Ibid., p. 181.

50 "modern and lighthearted approach". Ibid.

50 "weight". Ibid.

52 "compact place". Diane Welebit, "From the Top," House & Garden, CLVIII:5 (1986), 241.

52 "traditional Boston features". Ibid., p. 211.

52 "newly germinated skyscrapers". Ibid.

56 "minor blast of blue". Welebit, op. cit.

58 "the character of [a room] comes from things around the upholstered pieces". Kunstel, op. cit., p. 62.

60 "downplayed". Interview with Gregory Richardson, September 21, 2010.

70 "so loved". Ibid.

70 "they insisted it be duplicated". Ibid.

72 "simplified the architecture". Susan Mary Alsop, "Under Bald Mountain," Architectural Digest, XLIII:12 (1986), 167.

72 "ruggedness of the architecture". Ibid., p. 168.

72 "essential element of the house". Ibid.

72 "everything [of his client's], and filling in where need be. He wastes nothing". Interview with Helaine Allen, September 23, 2010.

77 "Madame, have you forgotten that you have six dogs?" Interview with Sophie Engelhard, October 5, 2010.

78–80 "so faded and worn", "spare", "voluptuous". Joan Chatfield-Taylor, "Lyrical Interlude on Nob Hill," Architectural Digest, XLV:8 (1988), 185.

83 "romantic". Ibid.

84 "biggest job was making it look as though it belonged again, to create a design that was appropriate both for the 1916 building and [his clients]". Carol Vogel, "Time Stands Still," The New York Times Magazine, May 1, 1988, 103.

84 "an immediate view into the living room and to the cityscape outside". Ibid.

84 "stripped". Ibid.

87 "a pleasing informality". Michael Webb, "Boston Revival," Architectural Digest, LI:2 (1994), 144.

90 "sensible progression". Vogel, op. cit.

94 "reworked". Peter Carlsen, "Interior Landscapes," Architectural Digest, XLVI:8 (1989), 173.

94 "in the middle of the swellest horse country in America". Ibid.

94 "no interior architectural detailing". Fact & Credit Sheets, Courtesy of Architectural Digest and Condé Nast archives.

94 "more freedom to make changes without guilt". Carlsen, op. cit.

94 "[used] a classical vocabulary". Fact & Credit Sheets, Courtesy of Architectural Digest and Condé Nast archives.

94 "strong architectural elements". Ibid.

94 "level of detail, quality and precision". Interview with Hodgins's client, October 24, 2010.

94 "over the course of so many months". e-mail from Hodgins's client, August 1, 2012.

94 "to put the house in use". Interview with William Hodgins, December 29, 2010.

94 "extraordinary". e-mail from Hodgins's client, August 1, 2012.

94 "to let them share their creation with their loved ones." Ibid.

96 "swelled out and crumpled onto the [original wide plank pine] floor". Carlsen, op. cit., p. 174.

96 "edited color palette". Fact & Credit Sheets, Courtesy of Architectural Digest and Condé Nast archives.

100 "soft glow". Carlsen, op. cit., p. 176.

100 "glamorously pared-down". Ibid.

103 "separate wing of the house for casual living". Fact & Credit Sheets, Courtesy of Architectural Digest and Condé Nast archives.

103 "Italian-monastic feeling of the paneled room gave the client a slightly whimsical retreat from the more classical restraint in the other part of the house". Fact & Credit Sheets, Courtesy of Architectural Digest and Condé Nast archives.

103 "grand and rustically simple details". Carlsen, op. cit., p. 178.

103 "slight wash of uneven color". Fact & Credit Sheets, Courtesy of Architectural Digest and Condé Nast archives.

104 "had the best time". Interview with Roz Gould, December 28, 2010.

110 "consulted". Elizabeth H. Hunter, "Treasuring the Past," House Beautiful, CXXXII:1 (1990), 48.

110 "smitten". Ibid.

110 "cottage". Ibid.

110 "long before the Lloyds bought [it]. He used to drive by [the house] and think what wonderful windows!" Ibid.

110 "match the elegance of the rooms". Ibid., p. 52.

110 "let light into the rooms beyond". Ibid.

110 "barely noticeable"—"just a whisper". Ibid.

110 "old-world elegance". Ibid.

110 "romantic". Ibid., p. 52.

112 "peculiar". Ibid., p. 51.

112 "way off-center". Ibid.

112 "create intimacy and focus on the fireplace". Carol Cooper Garey, House Beautiful: Decorating Style (New York: Hearst Books, 1992), p. 49.

112 "recessive". Hunter, op. cit.

114 "old painted finishes". Ibid. p. 55.

114 "weight" and "contrast". Ibid.

116 "Black Box". Interview with Charlene Engelhard, June 16, 2012.

116 "depressing". Ibid.

116 "all light". Ibid.

116 "[unusual] conglomeration of furniture". Postel and Brox, op. cit., p. 50.

116 "loves the impromptu, [and] has a talent for it. If she [likes] something, that [is] it". Lawford, op. cit., p. 56.

116 "go beyond anything you could ever expect. He's got that great eye and finds you great stuff. [Experiencing his rooms] is like walking into a painting. It's like Christmas. You can't believe you live there". Interview with Charlene Engelhard, January 27, 2011.

122 "a mixture of everything". Fact & Credit Sheets, June 23, 1980, Courtesy of Architectural Digest and Condé Nast archives.

128 "medium-size". Simpson, op. cit., p. 192.

128 "character". Ibid.

128 "very difficult". Ibid.

128 "elegance on this [intimate] scale". Ibid.

128 "older, grander houses". Ibid.

128 "pale and musty painting of dropped white linen after the Empire style". Ibid.

128 "feel special and different from the rest of the apartment". Ibid.

128 "softest green". Ibid.

128 "edited and re-used". Fact & Credit Sheets, March 5, 1990, Courtesy of *Architectural Digest* and Condé Nast archives.

128 "divinely airy". Simpson, op. cit., p. 189.

128 "uniformly pristine decoration in every shade of white, from ecru to ivory, from eggshell to bone". Ibid.

130 "flowed gently". Ibid., p. 191.

132 "palest". Fact & Credit Sheets, March 5, 1990, Courtesy of *Architectural Digest* and Condé Nast archives.

133 "Korean-style". Ibid.

136 "specially colored". Fact & Credit Sheets, Courtesy of *Architectural Digest* and Condé Nast archives, op. cit.

136 "last finishing touch". Interview with Penny Matteson, August 20, 2012.

138 "[softened] the periphery of [the] room". Pittel, op. cit., p. 35.

138 "chipped and flakey painted finishes". Ibid., p. 38.

138 "crudeness". Ibid.

140 "set the character of a room". Presentation by William Hodgins, *Architectural Digest* symposium at The Smithsonian Institution, Washington, D.C., May 7, 1990.

140 "created a clear, strong structure [in the living room] with sofa, coffee table, desk, huge urns and garden statue". Elizabeth H. Hunter, "William Hodgins in the City . . . And in the Country," *House Beautiful*, CXXXIII:10 (1991), 79.

144 "regularity, rhythm and a sense of architectural completeness". Fact & Credit Sheets, June 18, 1991, Courtesy of *Architectural Digest* and Condé Nast archives.

144 "to say how much he loved". Interview with Helaine Allen, September 23, 2010.

146 "luxurious simplicity". Suzanne Stephens, "White Heat for Palm Beach," *Architectural Digest*, XLVIII:11 (1991), 140.

146 "slightly strong formal shape contrasted with the pale colors". Cregan, op. cit.

148 "park like". Fact & Credit Sheets, Courtesy of *Architectural Digest* and Condé Nast archives.

148 "without a word to her husband". William Weaver, "Stable Comforts in Southampton," *Architectural Digest*, L:4 (1993), 109.

148 "its openness and airy scale". Fact & Credit Sheets, Courtesy of *Architectural Digest* and Condé Nast archives.

148 "considered ideal". Michael Webb, "The View from Martha's Vineyard," LI:6 (1994), 109.

148 "made a wide and welcoming entrance hall, keeping the sense that the building was originally a stable". Fact & Credit Sheets, Courtesy of *Architectural Digest* and Condé Nast archives.

148 "where saddles were once racked". Weaver, op. cit.

150 "intimate, comfortable and welcoming". Ibid., p. 104.

150 "simple [but substantial] lengths". Ibid., p. 109.

153 "a casual and comfortable dining area—good to look at and easy to use without completely overtaking the room". Fact & Credit Sheets, Courtesy of *Architectural Digest* and Condé Nast archives.

153 "massive sliding [stable] doors". Weaver, op. cit., p. 109.

153 "blackened to underline their presence". Ibid.

153 "gentle, old-fashioned". Ibid., p. 111.

153 "(favored by Mr. Rohatyn)". Interview with Elizabeth Rohatyn, July 24, 2010.

154 "knit [the house] back together". Michael Webb, "Boston Revival," *Architectural Digest*, LI:2 (1994), 145.

154 "dummy wall". Ibid., p. 146.

154 "(Hodgins told Willard he could have any color he wanted as long as it was a shade of white)". Interview with Ralph Willard, September 29, 2010.

154 "to give scale to the walls". Webb, op. cit.

154 "park bench". Interview with Penny Matteson, April 1, 2011.

156 "he and Robert Blankenship meticulously curtained". Interview with Penny Matteson, April 1, 2011.

156 "air of a proscenium arch". Webb, op. cit.

157 "it encourages people to talk and creates a pleasing informality". Webb, op. cit., p. 144.

159 "quietly elegant". Fact & Credit Sheets, May 5, 1992, Courtesy of *Architectural Digest* and Condé Nast archives.

159 "properly Bostonian in its understated sense of period". Webb, op. cit., p. 147.

160 "bland". Elizabeth H. Hunter, "Life at The Ritz," *House Beautiful*, CXXXIX:5 (1997), 108.

160 "brightest of eight white paint formulas in his repertoire". Ibid., p. 109.

160 "fool the eye". Ibid.

160 "the contemporary feel of the apartment". Ibid.

160 "a modern shell for [his] old things". Ibid.

166 "large, but has the simplicity and warmth of an American country cabin". Verlyn Klinkenborg, "Homestead Style in Wyoming," *Architectural Digest*, LIV:6 (1997), 178.

166 "was to adapt the rough-hewn look of log homestead buildings to the needs of Mr. and Mrs. Rohatyn, whose lives are anything but rough-hewn". Ibid., p. 181.

166 "sympathetic to the rest of the compound". Ibid.

166 "to be as un-chichi as possible". Ibid., p. 179.

166 "a soft, slightly driftwood look". Ibid., p. 185.

166 "huge deep sofas". Fact & Credit Sheets, Courtesy of *Architectural Digest* and Condé Nast archives.

169 "bright, old, slightly worn red". Courtesy of William Hodgins Incorporated.

169 "meant for restaurant use". Fact & Credit Sheets, Courtesy of *Architectural Digest* and Condé Nast archives.

169 "the extraordinary views of landscape". Klinkenborg, op. cit., p. 179.

169 "requested by Mr. and Mrs. Rohatyn". Fact & Credit Sheets, Courtesy of *Architectural Digest* and Condé Nast archives.

170 "differentiated [the bedroom] from the rest of the house". Klinkenborg, op. cit., p. 182.

170 "a quiet, private place to read, work or have tea". Fact & Credit Sheets, Courtesy of *Architectural Digest* and Condé Nast archives.

172 "Tranquility," derived from "shifting hues of off-white, soft putty, and stone". Lance Esplund, "Well Dressed & Fashionably Pale," *House & Garden*, CLXVII:1 (1998), 96.

172 "stripped the building of Victorian accre-

tions, and designed a seamless, two-story, L-shaped addition". Ibid., p. 98.

174 "dwarfed". Ibid., p. 96.

174 "conventional". Ibid., p. 95.

174 "who had a [major] hand in the interiors". Ibid.

174 "nuances in temperature and texture, more than in hue, [that] become apparent with each change in light". Ibid., p. 96.

177 "range of textures and shades of white in the master bedroom [that was] as subtle as it [was] dramatic". Ibid., p. 100.

178 "Hodgins talks to architects, builders, and tradesmen in their own language". Interview with Joan Daniels, September 26, 2010.

178 "to do it his way, at his degree of precision and detail". Interview with Hodgins's client, October 24, 2010.

178 "labors over their work". Interview with Henry Reeder, October 21, 2010.

178 "pushes them to new heights. They in turn have enormous respect for Hodgins and learn from him". Interview with Hodgins's client, October 24, 2010.

178 "palette of soft, pretty colors". Elizabeth H. Hunter, "Seaside Sensibility," *House Beautiful*, CXXXIX:7 (1997), 67.

178 "supremely comfortable". Ibid.

178 "This house makes you feel good". Ibid.

183 "Nantucket-style". Courtesy of William Hodgins Incorporated.

184 "and respected what he represented". Interview with Laura Munder, September 20, 2010.

184 "it needed everything". Ibid.

184 "very old-world, formal". Daphne Nikolopoulos, "Family Matters," *Palm Beach Illustrated*, LV:2 (2006), 167–168.

184 "strong architecture". Martin Filler, "Palm Beach Story," *House Beautiful*, CXLII:12 (2000), 126.

184 "made the [oceanfront] room seem taller and more elegant". e-mail from Lucien Allaire, April 28, 2011.

184 "very, very deeply stained dark brown". Ibid.

184 "This was how she wanted the house to feel". Interview with Laura Munder, September 20, 2010.

186 "luxury of ordering furniture from Morocco". Filler, op. cit., p. 127.

188 "taste and style". Agnes Sarah Clark, "Color and Light," *Veranda*, XIII:3 (1999), 122.

188 "graceful". Ibid.

188 "amplified moldings and added cornices". Ibid.

188 "softly marbleized". Fact & Credit Sheets, Courtesy of *Architectural Digest* and Condé Nast archives.

210 "an enchanting pale blue glazed cotton chintz patterned in off-white swags of lace embracing stylized bouquets of multicolored roses and fuchsia in each of its respective bows". Courtesy of Dessin Fournir.

212 "on a piece of land that was originally part of George Washington's farm". Susan Sheehan, "The Art of the Retreat," *Architectural Digest*, LX:3 (2003), 180.

212 "a world away". Interview with Hodgins's client, October 24, 2010.

212 "down the bumpy dirt road that [lead] to the house". Sheehan, "The Art of the Retreat."

212 "could be in New England". Ibid.

212 "walls that had [closed] up the downstairs rooms". Ibid.

212 "Existing windows and doors were replaced

by almost floor-to-ceiling French windows and doors". Ibid.

212 "Classic cornices and moldings were added, and the first-floor ceilings were raised fourteen inches". Ibid.

213 "loves [gentle] colors more than anyone [he's] ever worked for". Ibid., p. 185.

214 "uneven". Sheehan, "The Art of the Retreat," p. 183.

214 "for their shape". Ibid.

215 "special". Sheehan, "The Art of the Retreat."

215 "tiny apartment". Interview with Hodgins's client, October 24, 2010.

217 "filmy, dreamlike". Sheehan, "The Art of the Retreat," p. 186.

217 "to emphasize its architectural character." Ibid.

218 "to just do it!" Interview with Carolyn Hyman, August 25, 2010.

220 "bird-and-branch". Courtesy of Lee Jofa.

224 "a sense of tradition, of belonging". Cregan, op. cit.

224 "enfilade". Ibid.

224 "so they [glowed]". Ibid.

226 "beige is a bright color to [me]". Interview with Hodgins's client, October 24, 2010.

226 "slightly strong formal [shape]". Cregan, op. cit.

230 "A lot of people come to [his] firm for [that reason]". Hunter, op. cit., p. 109.

232 "strong carved legs" and "awkward-looking [lions' paw] feet". Cregan, op. cit.

235 "finds white the most comforting color for a bedroom". Cregan, op. cit., p. 46.

235 "fine gradations of white". Ibid.

240 wanted a very pale apartment" with "a white living room". Susan Sheehan, "Lighter Shade of Pale," *Architectural Digest*, LXIII:1 (2006), 138.

240 "without trepidation". Ibid.

240 "to keep mixing until the white wasn't simply white but white white white". Ibid.

246 "warmth". Ibid., p. 139.

248 "happy, sunny, yellow master bedroom". Ibid., p. 141.

260 "upholstered pieces must not only be comfortable, they must look comfortable". Interview with Bob Shannon, October 27, 2010.

264 "a classic look with no color and no fancies". Interview with Hodgins's client, September 27, 2010.

264 "gave it to them". Ibid.

264 "clean-line". Interview with Hodgins's client, September 27, 2010.

264 "raw space". Ibid.

264 "as much glass with sliders [the client] could get". Ibid.

264 "to create a little sparkle and direct the eye upwards". Interview with William Hodgins, July 14, 2012.

264 "he helped his client move from her house, used everything from there and [oversaw] it all in his fine, caring and gentlemanly manner". Interview with Hodgins's client, September 27, 2010.

264 "splayed out" and their upholstery "popped". Ibid.

268 "exacting placement". Ibid.

268 "give her rooms color". Ibid.

268 "classicism and modernity". "The World's Most Beautiful Fireplaces—The Soane Collection," at chesneys.com.

273 "shopped for" in the walk-in "secret closet" she "visited regularly". Interview with Hodgins's client, September 27, 2010.

273 "finds". Ibid.

274 "are both extreme perfectionists and it seems that they were both eager to be more audacious in the concept and aesthetic choices". e-mail from Lucien Allaire, March 9, 2011.

274 "not thought to be a permanent residence". Ibid.

274 "geared". Ibid.

274 "more experimental". Ibid.

274 "Modern". Ibid.

274 "is from a different generation, he still embraces all design with his masterful eye and puts it all together" with the "same elements of taste and quality". Ibid.

274 "catches light". Interview with Hodgins's client, March 15, 2011.

276 "perfect white-white". Allaire, op. cit.

276 "bleach-white". Courtesy of Leni's Inc.

276 "relationship of shape to shape, weights and textures". e-mail from Hodgins's client, March 15, 2011.

282 "femininity expressed in a very simple way". e-mail from Lucien Allaire, March 9, 2011.

284 "genius and done only as William Hodgins would do". Ibid.

284 "like a Kahr". Ibid.

284 "labeled the finish sample that [was] finally selected". Ibid.

286 "who had always wanted to feel like she was living in a New York penthouse". Interview with Alison Wintman, September 10, 2011.

286 "palest". Courtesy of William Hodgins Incorporated.

288 "strong" and dark wood pieces in his rooms. He places "that type of furniture next to white, and the white becomes weightier". Cregan, op. cit.

294 "use everything". Interview with Helaine Allen, September 23, 2010.

294 "crowding". Interview with Helaine Allen, October 22, 2011.

300 "depicting a playful and fanciful design of gibbons, birds and flora in an exotic subtropic fantasy". e-mail from John Howard, November 15, 2011.

304 "very difficult" time. Interview with Helaine Allen, September 23, 2010.

304 "pasted [material samples] on the bedroom wall, laid on the floor". Ibid.

304 "became annoyed" and told her to "select something!" Ibid.

304 "That's it!" Ibid.

304 "No, that's enough!" Ibid.

SELECTED CLIENTS

BOSTON, MASSACHUSETTS
Mr. and Mrs. Milton Abramson
Mrs. Helaine Allen
Mr. and Mrs. David Altschuler
Mrs. Janice Bacon
Prince Bandar Bin Khalid Al Faisal
 and Princess Nouf Abdullah
Mr. and Mrs. Melvin Barkan
Judge and Mrs. Matthew Brown
Mr. and Mrs. Austin Cable
Ms. Dee Dee Chereton
Mrs. Carol Cohen
Mr. and Mrs. Julian Cohen
Mr. and Mrs. J. Linzee Coolidge
Mr. and Mrs. Anton Effgen
Ms. Sophie Engelhard
Mr. and Mrs. Steven Feinberg
Mrs. Norma Fine
Mr. and Mrs. Monte Goldman
Mr. and Mrs. Calvin Gould
Mr. and Mrs. David Jones
Mr. and Mrs. Robert Keezer
Mr. and Mrs. Alan Leventhal
Mr. and Mrs. Phillip Lowe
Mr. and Mrs. Robert Monks
Mr. and Mrs. Abraham Moskow
Mr. and Mrs. Robert O'Block
Mr. and Mrs. Joseph Paresky
Ms. Sally Pingree
Mr. and Mrs. Herbert Richmond
Mr. and Mrs. Howard Rubin
Mr. and Mrs. Lawrence Schumann
Mr. and Mrs. Carl Shapiro
Mrs. Helen Spaulding
Ms. Tori Thomas
Mr. and Mrs. Arthur Waldstein
Mr. and Mrs. Stephen Weiner
Mr. Morgan Wheelock
Mr. and Mrs. Ralph Willard
Mrs. Audrey Wintman
Dr. Ira Yerkes

BROOKLINE, MASSACHUSETTS
Mrs. Patricia Black
Mr. and Mrs. Stanton Black
Mr. and Mrs. Charles Cunningham
Mr. and Mrs. Lee Daniels
Mr. and Mrs. Stephen Endlar
Mr. and Mrs. Philip Faneuil
Mr. and Mrs. Norman Feinberg
Mr. and Mrs. Thomas Frost
Mr. and Mrs. Morton Godine
Mr. and Mrs. Joseph Linsey
Mr. and Mrs. Lewis Lloyd
Mrs. Ruth Lockwood

Mr. and Mrs. Lester Morse
Mr. and Mrs. Richard Morse
Mr. and Mrs. Maynard Winston

CAMBRIDGE, MASSACHUSETTS
Mr. and Mrs. George P. Edmonds Jr.
Ms. Charlene Engelhard
Mr. and Mrs. Irving Glickman
Mrs. Rhonda Segal

CHESTNUT HILL, MASSACHUSETTS
Mr. and Mrs. Alvin Allen
Mr. and Mrs. David Altschuler
Mrs. Carol Feinberg
Mr. and Mrs. Joseph Fuller
Mr. and Mrs. Albert Levine
Mr. and Mrs. Joseph Linsey
Mr. Carl Martignetti
Mr. and Mrs. Robert O'Block
Mrs. Leila Perlmutter
Mr. and Mrs. J. Hunter Walton

NEWTON, MASSACHUSETTS
Mr. and Mrs. Leo Bakalar
Mr. and Mrs. Theodore Berenson
Mr. and Mrs. Norman Feinberg
Mr. and Mrs. Lester Mendelsohn
Mr. and Mrs. Mark O'Leary
Mrs. Leila Perlmutter
Mr. and Mrs. Samuel Rabinowitz
Mr. and Mrs. Daniel Rothenberg
Mr. and Mrs. Lester Sobin
Mr. and Mrs. Melvin Wintman

WEST NEWTON, MASSACHUSETTS
Mr. and Mrs. Alvin Allen
Mr. and Mrs. James Brilliant
Mr. and Mrs. Robert Keezer
Mr. and Mrs. Alan Leventhal
Mr. and Mrs. Irving Perlmutter
Mr. and Mrs. Lester Sobin
Mr. and Mrs. James Wood

WABAN, MASSACHUSETTS
Mr. and Mrs. Austin Cable
Mr. and Mrs. Donald Drourr
Mr. and Mrs. Leo Kahn

WELLESLEY, MASSACHUSETTS
Mr. and Mrs. Peter Bernon
Mr. and Mrs. Howard Grayson
Mr. and Mrs. Robert Smith

WESTON, MASSACHUSETTS
Mr. and Mrs. Mark Goldman
Mr. and Mrs. Robert Jaffe
Mr. and Mrs. Brian Knez
Mr. and Mrs. Neil Strauss
Mr. and Mrs. Ralph Willard
Mr. and Mrs. Burton Wynn

WAYLAND, MASSACHUSETTS
Mrs. Joan Berns
Mr. and Mrs. Steven Kaye

CONCORD, MASSACHUSETTS
Ms. Charlene Engelhard
Mr. and Mrs. Edward Redstone

DOVER, MASSACHUSETTS
Mr. and Mrs. Peter Bernon

LINCOLN, MASSACHUSETTS
Mr. and Mrs. William Scheft

WESTWOOD, MASSACHUSETTS
Mrs. Helen Spaulding

BEVERLY, MASSACHUSETTS
Mr. and Mrs. Norman Barron
Mr. and Mrs. Richard Humphrey
Mr. and Mrs. George Rimer
Mr. and Mrs. William Scheft
Mr. and Mrs. Christopher Weld

SWAMPSCOTT, MASSACHUSETTS
Mr. and Mrs. Leo Beckwith
Mr. and Mrs. Charles Feingold
Mr. and Mrs. Steven Lappin
Mr. and Mrs. Bruce Male
Mr. and Mrs. Louis Stahl

MARBLEHEAD, MASSACHUSETTS
Mr. and Mrs. Harvey Pastan

**MANCHESTER-BY-THE-SEA, MASSA-
CHUSETTS**
Mr. and Mrs. J. Linzee Coolidge
Mrs. Thomas Jefferson Coolidge
Mrs. Helen Spaulding

CAPE COD, MASSACHUSETTS
Mr. and Mrs. Julian Cohen
Mr. and Mrs. Lee Daniels
Mr. and Mrs. George P. Edmonds Jr.
Mr. and Mrs. Norman Feinberg
Mr. and Mrs. Alan Leventhal
Mr. and Mrs. Ralph Willard

MARTHA'S VINEYARD, MASSACHU-SETTS
Mr. and Mrs. William Graham

NANTUCKET, MASSACHUSETTS
Mr. and Mrs. Peter Bernon
Ms. Charlene Engelhard
Mr. and Mrs. Stephen Graham

PAXTON, MASSACHUSETTS
Mr. and Mrs. Stephen McDonough

STOCKBRIDGE, MASSACHUSETTS
Mr. and Mrs. Ralph Willard

RHODE ISLAND
Mrs. Oatsie Charles
Mr. and Mrs. E. Taylor Chewning Jr.
Mr. and Mrs. Bryce Hall
Mr. Richard Loebs Jr.
Mr. and Mrs. Joseph Sinclair

MAINE
Ms. Carol Beckwith
Mr. and Mrs. Julian Cohen
Mr. and Mrs. Peter Haffenreffer
Mr. and Mrs. Bernard Lewis
Mr. and Mrs. Robert Monks
Mr. and Mrs. J. Hunter Walton

WOODSTOCK, VERMONT
Mr. and Mrs. Brian Knez

CONNECTICUT
Mr. and Mrs. Edward Carpenter
Mr. and Mrs. Stephen Graham
Ms. Mary Matheson

NEW YORK, NEW YORK
Dr. and Mrs. Daniel Baker
Mr. Scott Bessent
Mr. and Mrs. Stephen Graham
Mr. and Mrs. Edward Hyman Jr.
Mr. and Mrs. Gerard Manolvicci
Ms. Mary Matheson
Mr. and Mrs. Felix Rohatyn
Ms. Jennifer Segal

THE HAMPTONS, NEW YORK
Mr. and Mrs. Robert O'Block
Ms. Sally Pingree
Mr. and Mrs. Felix Rohatyn
Mr. and Mrs. Eugene Williams Jr.

FIRE ISLAND, NEW YORK
Mr. and Mrs. Edward Hyman Jr.

FISHERS ISLAND, NEW YORK
Mr. and Mrs. Edward Carpenter

AVALON, NEW JERSEY
Mr. and Mrs. Myung Song

GLADWYNE, PENNSYLVANIA
Mr. and Mrs. Myung Song

EASTERN SHORE, MARYLAND
Mr. and Mrs. Sumner Pingree
Mr. and Mrs. Albert Van Metre

WASHINGTON, D.C.
Mrs. Henry Brandon
Mr. and Mrs. E. Taylor Chewning Jr.
Ms. Sophie Engelhard
Mr. and Mrs. Robert Monks
Ms. Sally Pingree
Ms. Leslie Stahl
Ms. Tori Thomas

VIRGINIA
Mrs. Mary Chewning
Ms. Sophie Engelhard
Mr. and Mrs. John Hanes
Mrs. Catherine Winkler Herman
Ms. Tori Thomas

SHEPHERDSTOWN, WEST VIRGINIA
Mr. and Mrs. John Hanes

ALBANY, GEORGIA
Mr. and Mrs. Eugene Williams Jr.

PALM BEACH, FLORIDA
Mr. and Mrs. Alvin Allen
Mr. and Mrs. Leo Beckwith
Mr. and Mrs. Peter Bernon
Mr. and Mrs. Austin Cable
Mrs. Carol Cohen
Mr. and Mrs. Julian Cohen
Mr. and Mrs. Lee Daniels
Mrs. Florence Eisner
Mr. and Mrs. Norman Feinberg
Mr. and Mrs. Calvin Gould
Mr. and Mrs. Howard Grayson
Mr. and Mrs. Joseph Linsey
Mr. and Mrs. Robert Monks
Mr. and Mrs. Lee Munder
Mr. and Mrs. Carl Shapiro
Mr. and Mrs. Samuel Shapiro
Mr. and Mrs. Melvin Wintman

HOBE SOUND, FLORIDA
Mr. and Mrs. Edward Carpenter
Mrs. Helen Spaulding

DELRAY, FLORIDA
Mr. and Mrs. Norman Barron
Mr. and Mrs. Lester Sobin

BOCA RATON, FLORIDA
Mr. and Mrs. Lee Daniels
Mr. and Mrs. Myung Song

TALLAHASSEE, FLORIDA
Mr. and Mrs. Frederic Hamilton

BIRMINGHAM, MICHIGAN
Mr. and Mrs. Lee Munder

BLOOMFIELD HILLS, MICHIGAN
Mr. and Mrs. Lee Munder
Mr. and Mrs. Robert Taubman

LADUE, MISSOURI
Mr. and Mrs. Eugene Williams Jr.

CORA, WYOMING
Mr. and Mrs. Felix Rohatyn

MONTANA
Mr. and Mrs. John Hanes
Mr. and Mrs. Robert Smith

SUN VALLEY, IDAHO
Ms. Sophie Engelhard
Ms. Tori Thomas

SAN FRANCISCO, CALIFORNIA
Mr. and Mrs. Robert Taubman

DORADO BEACH, PUERTO RICO
Mr. and Mrs. Monte Goldman

GRAND CAYMAN ISLAND
Mr. and Mrs. Philip Lowe

NEVIS, WEST INDIES
Mr. and Mrs. Julian Cohen

PARIS, FRANCE
Ambassador and Mrs. Felix Rohatyn

RIYADH, SAUDI ARABIA
Prince Bandar Bin Khalid Al Faisal
  and Princess Nouf Abdullah

PUBLIC COMMISSIONS
AIDS Hospice at Mission Hill
  Roxbury, Massachusetts
Augusta National
  Augusta, Georgia
Fenway Health
  Boston, Massachusetts
Keeneland Association
  Lexington, Kentucky
Rockwell House
  Dorchester, Massachusetts
Sotheby Parke Bernet
  Boston, Massachusetts
Taunton Dog Track
  Raynham, Massachusetts
Wang Center; visitors' room
  Boston, Massachusetts
Willow Bend Country Club;
  model home
  Mashpee, Massachusetts

AFTERWORD AND ACKNOWLEDGMENTS

Since childhood, I have been passionate about art, architecture, and interior design. My parents, grandparents, and great-grandmother exposed me to wonderful antiques and classically beautiful interiors in their own homes. My parents took me and my sister Susan, often "kicking and screaming," to theater, symphony, and the great museums in our hometown of Boston, and in New York where our paternal grandmother lived. In Boston, we frequently visited the Museum of Fine Arts where our mother, June, always showed us one of her favorite paintings—Renoir's *Dance at Bougival*—to the Isabella Stewart Gardner Museum designed in the style of a fifteenth-century Venetian palace, and to performances of the Boston Pops conducted by Arthur Fiedler. I relished our visits to Boston's famed Newbury Street, where our mother took us to art galleries. She engaged Susan and me in looking at editioned prints by contemporary American artists and educated us about printmaking techniques and proper framing. Susan and I both became hooked on contemporary art, which has been a major part of our lives.

Newbury Street was also once home to William Hodgins Incorporated. Bill had moved from New York to Boston in 1968, when I was thirteen years old, and his notable reputation as a great decorator spread through the city like wildflowers. Many families our family knew hired him to decorate their homes and his classic, understated style quietly advanced design in the patrician city. Boston had good decorators, but Bill's work was special.

Although I saw a good deal of Bill's decorating in interior design magazines—*Architectural Digest, House & Garden,* and *House Beautiful*—it wasn't until 1984 that I met him and was actually face-to-face with his "design genius." Ellen Gordon, my good friend, invited me to dinner at the Palm Beach home of her mother and stepfather—Eunice and Julian Cohen. It was a pleasurable occasion to spend time with Ellen, reconnect with the Cohens who knew my family in Boston, and meet Bill Hodgins, also a dinner guest. Meeting Bill at the same time I was exposed personally to the superlative decorating and interior architecture he realized in the Cohen's Palm Beach regency-style house was a defining moment for me. When I walked into the house's majestic but quietly elegant living room, with its luxurious color palette in the palest shades of blue, cream, and beige, I knew viscerally that it was one of the most beautiful, tasteful, and welcoming rooms I would ever be in. The living room, which is featured in this book, is an interior that remains indelible in my mind to this day.

I did not interact with Bill again until 2000 when my first book, *The Country Houses of David Adler*, was going to press. I wrote Bill a letter, reminded him of our long-ago introduction, and asked him if he would read the proofs of the book and write a review of it for the book jacket. He graciously accepted the invitation and his thoughtfully composed review graces the back cover.

During the past twelve years, Bill and I have become good friends. Early on in our friendship, I suggested to him that a book be written about his decorating. It's something I believed in wholeheartedly, but as a newly published author at the time, I questioned if I would ever have the opportunity to write a book about his work. But in the past eight years, I have been fortunate to write and have published two books about revolutionary interior designers in America—*Frances Elkins: Interior Design* and *Michael Taylor: Interior Design*—also with the support, guidance, and encouragement of Nancy Green, my terrific editor at W. W. Norton & Company.

In 2010, Bill and I resumed our long-ago conversation about my writing a book about his work. I proposed the subject to Nancy and, naturally, Bill and I were very pleased when Norton's board accepted my book proposal and agreed to publish *William Hodgins Interiors.*

Researching for and writing the book about Bill Hodgins has been one of the most rewarding and fulfilling labors of love for me. Getting to know Bill even better and spending time with him—both in person and on the telephone—has strengthened our friendship and my appreciation for his "design genius." He is an Old World gentleman of admirable qualities who taught me that restraint can be applied to all phases of life, including my own writing. I admire Bill's low-key style and value and respect his high standards. All in all, I had a wonderful time!

I had the pleasure and privilege of spending quality time at Bill's office, working closely with him and his longstanding, devoted, and hard-working senior designer Penny Matteson and efficient and competent office manager Karen Hess. Both Penny and Karen patiently and diplomatically fielded endless e-mails, telephone calls, and letters from me requesting forty-plus years of William Hodgins Incorporated documentation I needed for the book.

Former design assistants at William Hodgins Incorporated, including Lucien Allaire, Paul Lanoix, Henry Petterson, Gregory Richardson, Robert Wrubel, and the late Richard Burke, were extremely generous with their time, insight, recollections of commissions, and appreciation of "Mr. Hodgins" and his talent. They supported me and my steadfast passion and commitment to writing the book.

I appreciate the help of Bill's Aunt Patricia Barré, his late mother's youngest sister, who lives in London, Ontario. Pat and I spoke often and her kind, gentle, and engaging personality and adoration of Bill contributed a great deal of love, warmth, and soul to the book. Donnie Lewis, Bill's good friend, at the outset of this project and before we even met, confirmed with me by telephone my intention that Sam, Bill's adored tricolor English springer spaniel and a major persona in his life and at the office, would be acknowledged in the book. Donnie encouraged me and contributed congenially to many of my visits with Bill, including a December morning when I interviewed Bill while the three of us ate breakfast at one of his favorite restaurants—the luncheonette at Green's Pharmacy in Palm Beach.

My sincere gratitude goes to Margaret Russell, editor-in-chief at *Architectural Digest*. In addition to writing the insightful and thoughtful Foreword, Margaret asked Shawn Waldron, archive director of the Condé Nast Archive, and Marianne Brown, the collections manager and assistant archivist, to locate the long-ago archived Fact & Credit Sheets that Bill routinely filled out for the magazine's editorial staff in preparation for each article it published on his work. The extensive records, which cover twenty of Bill's commissions spanning a period of twenty-five years, and meticulously identify all artwork, antiques, fabrics, and furniture (and their sources) featured in the articles, were fastidiously copied, organized, and packaged by Lauren Womack, an editorial assistant at *Architectural Digest*, and sent to me in Baltimore. Needless to say, the archival material is invaluable to the book, and Shawn, Marianne, and Lauren were immeasurably attentive and conscientious with their heady task.

Bill Hodgins's clients, many whom I have known since my childhood and are longstanding family friends, enthusiastically encouraged me and supported my project. They respected me and extended complete access to their homes and themselves, and expressed effusively their appreciation for Bill—both personally and professionally.

I am fortunate to have had access to numerous homes (several that Bill had photographed for the book) decorated by Bill, as well as many of his clients and their families who felt that he deserved to be honored and his work documented with a book. They are Helaine Allen, Teddy Berenson, Patricia Black, John Carney, Peter and Jane Carney, Edward and Mary Carpenter, Carol Feinberg Cohen, Lee and Joan Daniels, Annette de la Renta, Hope Edison, George P. and Sally Edmonds, Stephen and Alberta Endlar, Charlene Engelhard, Sophie Engelhard, Michael and Ellen Gordon, Roz Gould, John and Kiku Hanes, Edward and Caroline Hyman, Gracie Keezer, Debra Knez, Richard Loebs, Robert and Millicent Monks, Blanche Montesi, Lee and Laura Munder, Robert and Megan O'Block, Sally Pingree, Jane Rabb, Charlie and Natalie Reed, Marla Robinson, Felix and Elizabeth Rohatyn, Gitty Scheft, Rob and Dana Smith, Linda Taubman, Tori Thomas, Stephen and Roberta Weiner, Ralph Willard, Eugene and Evelyn Williams, and Alison Wintman.

I remember many friends, and former neighbors of my family's, who were Bill's clients, but are no longer living. I wish that each and every one of them could share in this tribute to him, including Alvin Allen, Lorraine Altschuler, Stanton Black, Austin and Marcia Cable, Julian and Eunice Cohen, Norman Feinberg, Robert Keezer, Philip and Carol Lowe, Irving and Leila Perlmutter, Norman and Eleanor Rabb, Ruth Shapiro, and Lester and Helen Sobin.

Bill Hodgins is greatly appreciated and respected by the professional associates he works with. They value his integrity, wonderful taste, and constructive guidance. I thank Sina Asta, Fred Browne, Jimmy Congema, Nick Crossley, Glen Dooley, Timothy Ewart, Anne Fairfax, Roy Hamilton, Daniel Harrison, Leni Joyce, Eric Kennedy, John Perry, Henry Reeder, Richard Sammons, Bob Shannon, Bob Sinclair, Christopher Spitzmiller, Franklin Tartaglione, Tony Victoria, and Jim Woolems for recollecting their interactions with him.

William Hodgins Interiors is composed of outstanding photography commensurate with his eloquent decorating. The book revels in the skill of many eminent photographers, including Gordon Beall, Antoine Bootz, Carmel Brantley, Julie Clayton, Billy Cunningham, Oberto Gili, Mick Hales, John Hall, Millicent Harvey, Lizzie Himmel, Michael Lee, Russell MacMasters, Jerry Rabinowitz, Laura Resen, Durston Saylor, Frederic Vasseur, and Peter Vitale.

Assembling, scanning, and preparing the archival material for the book would not have been possible without the diligence and commitment of Jeffrey Bauman, Marianne Brown, Audrey Chaney, Anne Fairfax, Pamela Gottfried, Nancy Hill, Kyle Hoepner, Karen Howes, Maggie Kasper, Justin Main, Cris McCarthy, Leigh Montville, Mike Poole, Paul Quitoriano, Linda Rye, Richard Sammons, Vivian Santangelo, Emily Schramm, Barbara von Schrieber, Newell Turner, and Shawn Waldron.

My family has been constantly supportive throughout all four book projects: my mother June and my late father Alan to whom I dedicate *William Hodgins Interiors*; my sister Susan, my brother-in-law Dean Trilling, their sons Scott and Andy and their wives, Meghan and Erin; and my great-niece and great-nephew, Elsie Rose and Adam, whom I love and cherish dearly. My late grandparents, Samuel Salny and Rae Salny Brown, and Jacob and Marion Freedman, and my late aunts, Edith Winetsky, and Barbara Hershenson, also influenced me.

Invaluable editorial guidance, friendship, and support came from Tristan and Mary Davies. Jessica Friedman shepherded me with sound legal and practical advice. Good friends have also been an important component to this project. Among these are Trudy and Mickey Magarill, who, for over thirty years have made my life in Baltimore warm, welcoming, comfortable, and fun; Robert Caro, Martin Gould, and John Winer who are lifelong friends; along with John Crocker, Cathy Lurie Cushing, Faye Florence, Eleanor Kress, Steve Levin, Janet Ludwig, Erica Stein, Sharyn Stein, Sheryl Stein, and Annie Stubbs. Susan Gordon and her son Teddy are dear friends, along with Jeff, Lynn, Sara, and Rachel Sachs. I also thank George Everly for his ongoing support and prudent guidance. I appreciate the support and friendship of Diane Ackerman, Rick Alexander, Kay Allaire, David Andelman, Paul and Leni Aronson, Jack and Louise Barber,

Barry and Connie Goodyear Baron, Jane Baum, Wayne and Susan Benjamin, John Berenson, Ruth Bernstein, Stuart and Wilma Bernstein, Lynn Beyer, Michael Billings, Trinity Bivalacqua, Joe Boccuzzi, Louis Bofferding, Diane Bower, Frances Bowes, David Boyd, Katherine Boyd, Bill Brockschmidt, Gertrude Brown, Judy Brown, Peter Bruun, Mario Buatta, Larry and Pam Burman, Connie Caplan, Denise Carberry, Harold Caro, Marilyn Caro, Edward Lee Cave, Bob Chandler, Dudley Clendinen, Whitney Clendinen, Courtney Coleman, Jeff Conti, Rosemary Cowler, Rosalie Dana, Dick and Rosalee Davison, Mark Dees, Brian Dermitt, John and Missy Derse, Daniel Detorie, Richard Dragisic, John Drum, Larry Dumont, Jennifer Duncan, Tony Duquette, Kay Evans, Charles Fair, Charles Fair Jr., George Farias, Pat and Cantey Ferchill, Ellen Fine, Alvan and Lois Finn, Beverly Fish, Jerry and Betty Fischbein, Roy and Joan Flesh, Audrey Foster, Melissa Gagen, Gil Garfield, John Gerald, Joe and Alma Gildenhorn, Joe Gillach, John Gilmer, Jimmy and Shelley Gitomer, Gail Glasser, Sally Gold, Sheldon and Shelley Goldseker, Ginger Gomprecht, Chissa Gordon, Philip Gorrivan, Lennie Greenberg, Leonard and Lois Greenebaum, Marjorie Greenebaum, Geoffrey and Maureen Lefton-Greif, Ayn Grinstein, Larry and Rita Guffey, Agnes Gund, Ann Gund, Paul Gunther, Ed Gunts, Albert Hadley, Elsbeth Haladay, David Hall, Thomas Hamel, Alexa Hampton, Mark and Duane Hampton, Michael Hampton, Ed Hardy, Leonard and Fleur Harlan, John and Peggy Heller, John and Carol Hess, Mike Hiles, Betty Jean Himeless, Alfie and Dana Himmelrich, Sam and Barbara Himmelrich, Larry Horn, Deke and Jeanne Jackson, Sandy and Anne Jacobson, Cathy Jakum, Cris Janoff, Jack Jarzavek, Marie Denise Jean, Charlie Johnston, Bill and Mimi Kahn, Larry and Evelyn Kamanitz, David Kanter, Myrna Kaplan, Louis Kates, Buddy and Linda Kaufman, Elliott and Fruema Klorfein, Virginia Knowles, Elie Kraut, Cary and Lisa Kravet, Ronald and Jo Carole Lauder, Douglas Levine, Adam Lewis, Maggie Lidz, Ron and Barbara Lipman, Don Ludwig, Wendy Luers, David and Bobbie Lundstrum, Fred Lyon, Carol Mack, Russell MacMasters, Jay Marc, Herb and Susan Marcus, Jane Marion, Nancy Lurie Marks, Tim Marks, Roth Martin, Tom and Danit Marton, Christopher Mason, Paul Mateyunas, Tom Mayer, Donald and Karine McCall, Will McGaul, Patti Menkes, Ann Miller, Phyllis Miller, Bill and Roseanna Milner, Joe Minton, Vernon Myers, Marc and Jane Nathanson, Leonard and Carol Nectow, David Netto, Judy Ney, Karen Nickey, Joe Nye, Liz O'Brien, Cait O'Connor, Steve Oney, Mitchell Owens, William Pahlmann, Bret Parsons, Leonard Pazulski, Jill Petschek, Zeke Phillips, Glen Piekarski, Philip and Harriet Plyler, Nancy Porter, Scott Powell, Scott and Lori Pugatch, Eden Rafshoon, Emily Wei Rales, Mark Reader, Peter Reed, Bob and Ruth Remis, Fred and Suzanne Rheinstein, Rick Robertson, Stan Rodbell, Bonnie Rogers, Todd Romano, Marilyn Rosenthal, Penny Rozis, Ed and Vicki Rubin, Al Ruschmeyer, Marjorie Salter, Judy Sandler, Vicki Sant, Mark and Debbie Saran, Tom Savage, Gil Schafer, Stuart and Barbara Schaftel, Nick Schloeder, Tommy and Claire Segal, Harvey Segaloff, Ben and Rosalie Shapero, Sig and Barbara Shapiro, Mark Sikes, Ben Simon, Susan Slayton, Elaine Spero, Brad and Melissa Spring, Chris Spring, Rob Stanford, Sherman Starr, Herb and Renie Stein, Robert Steloff, Robert A. M. Stern, Sheldon Stern, Madeline Stuart, Rose Tarlow, Henrika Taylor, Tommy and Lee Touchton, Charlotte Triefus, Suzanne Tucker, Elizabeth Van Ella, Max von der Decken, Janie Wagner, Darren Walker, Phyllis Washington, Kelly Weinreb, Carol Weis, Hutton and Ruth Wilkinson, Dede Wilsey, Mike and Marilyn Winer, Calvin Yeung, Christian Zanev, Lloyd Zuckerberg, Roy Zuckerberg, and Elliot Zulver.

I also appreciate the following people who helped and supported me during the research for this book: Stanley Abercrombie, Susan Adland, Emelie Alexander, Janice Alexander, Christie Ayres, Jacques Bailly, Cathy Balshone, Chris Bentley, Michael Berens, Michael Boodro, Audrey Brandon, Maggie Brooks, David Campbell, Debra Carattoni, Dawn Carlson, Cynthia Cathcart, Sarah Cecil, Lynn Chase, Chyanne Chutkow, Celeste Cooper, Jan Currie, Linda Degeorges, Sharon Dehmer, Denise Digianvittorio, Peter Duchin, Terry Duffy, James Duncan, Carol Eberts, Laurie Ellis, Pamela Fox, Stan Friedman, Allie Garcy, Anna Garling, Rebecca Garner, Melisa Gagen, Danny Gonzalez, Tom Graham, Beth Greene, Lisa Greenhouse, Meg Gurs, John Harding, Christa Hartsock, Sarah Heineman, Kirstin Hellwig, Cameron Henderson, Angela Henville, Rachel Herbert, Tom Hilditch, Carrie Hojnicki, Masie Houghton, John Howard, Christ Jean, Robyn Jensen, Eileen Jones, Meghan Jones, Eve Kahn, Alan Kerns, Margaret Kiechefer, Mary Kooi, Peter Lang, Linda Leahy, Maggie Lidz, Rolph Lippuner, Kingsley Lynch, Lorraine Lynch, Kara MacIntyre, Tom Marshall, Richard Maurer, Doris Maysonet, Merrick McMahon, Susan Minobe, Greg Mitchell, Lindsey Morris, Lisa Mosher, Mario Moura, Donna Neligon, Eleanor Niermann, Janet Oberto, Andrew Ogletree, Florence Palomo, Connie Parker, Kristen Patten, Louis Postel, John Raup, Shax Riegler, Elsie Riggins, Missy Rinfret, Peter Rose, Ken Savinski, Henry Scannell, Wendy Scheir, Marvin and Lee Schorr, Aaron Siegel, Charles Spada, Arnold Steinberg, Michael Stier, Judy Straeten, Amanda Strauss, Jeanne Swadosh, Michael Tammaro, Isabel Toolsie, Vicki Vanewalt, Pilar Viladis, Athena Waligore, Pat Ward, Charlotte Weidlein, Dale Wilson, Vicente Wolf, and Michael Wollaeger.

At W. W. Norton, I thank Nancy Green for her continual professionalism, enthusiasm, and encouragement of my passion and writing; Kevin Olsen, marketing director; Ben Yarling, editorial assistant; Carol Rose, copy editor; and Abigail Sturges, designer, whose collaborative input always creates a book with tremendous aesthetic appeal.

Franz Schulze, my Lake Forest College art and architectural history professor, mentor, and good friend told me thirty-five years ago that the independent study I conducted under his auspices on great house architect David Adler would one day be a book. Because of Franz's initial and ongoing confidence in me, I now introduce *William Hodgins Interiors*, my fourth book.

PHOTO CREDITS

1. (top) © Karen Radkai; (bottom) signature courtesy of William Hodgins.
2. © Millicent Harvey Photography
7. Harry Benson/*Architectural Digest* © 2007 Condé Nast Publications, Inc. Reprinted by permission. All Rights Reserved.
8. Courtesy of William Hodgins Inc.
9. Lizzie Himmel
11–13. Reprinted with permission of *House Beautiful* © 1971.
14. David Massey/*House & Garden* © 1972 Condé Nast Publications. Reprinted by permission. All Rights Reserved.
15. (top left) Ernst Beadle/*House & Garden* © 1972 Condé Nast Publications, Inc. Reprinted by permission. All Rights Reserved; (top right) David Massey/*House & Garden* © 1972 Condé Nast Publications, Inc. Reprinted by permission. All Rights Reserved; (bottom) Kevin J. Shea, courtesy of William Hodgins Inc.
16. Courtesy of William Hodgins Inc.
17–18. Horst P. Horst/*Architectural Digest* © 1981 Condé Nast Publications, Inc. Reprinted by permission. All Rights Reserved.
19–21. Johann Mayr/*Architectural Digest* © 1981 Condé Nast Publications, Inc. Reprinted by permission. All Rights Reserved.
22. Antoine Bootz
23–24. Lizzie Himmel
25. Jacques Dirand/The Interior Archive
26–29. Oberto Gili/*Vogue* © 1986 Condé Nast Publications, Inc. Reprinted by permission. All Rights Reserved.
31–35. Marina Faust/*Architectural Digest* © 1998 Condé Nast Publications, Inc. Reprinted by permission. All Rights Reserved.
37. Photo by Russ Rocknak, courtesy of *New England Home*
38–43. Peter Vitale/*Architectural Digest* © 1983 Condé Nast Publications, Inc. Reprinted by permission. All Rights Reserved.
44–46. Joseph Standart/*Architectural Digest* © 1984 Condé Nast Publications, Inc. Reprinted by permission. All Rights Reserved.
47. Joseph Standart
48–51. Peter Vitale/*Architectural Digest* © 1982 Condé Nast Publications, Inc. Reprinted by permission. All Rights Reserved.
52–57. Mick Hales
58. Courtesy of William Hodgins Inc.
59–63. Photo by Julie Carpenter, courtesy of Pamela H. Gottfried.
64. (left) Courtesy of William Hodgins Inc.
64(right)–69. Photo by Julie Carpenter, courtesy of Pamela H. Gottfried.
70–71. Courtesy of William Hodgins Inc.
72–83. Russell MacMasters Photography
84–93. Lizzie Himmel
94–103. Antoine Bootz
104–109. Carmel Brantley, Brantley Photography.
110–115. Reprinted with permission of *House Beautiful* © 1990.
116–127. Antoine Bootz
128–131. Antoine Bootz/*Architectural Digest* © 1990 Condé Nast Publications, Inc. Reprinted by permission. All Rights Reserved.
132. Antoine Bootz
133-136. Antoine Bootz/*Architectural Digest* © 1990 Condé Nast Publications, Inc. Reprinted by permission. All Rights Reserved.
137–143. Antoine Bootz
144–147. Carlos Domenech/*Architectural Digest* © 1991 Condé Nast Publications, Inc. Reprinted by permission. All Rights Reserved.
148–153. David Phelps/*Architectural Digest* © 1993 Condé Nast Publications, Inc. Reprinted by permission. All Rights Reserved.
154–159. Richard Mandelkorn/*Architectural Digest* © 1994 Condé Nast Publications, Inc. Reprinted by permission. All Rights Reserved.
160–165. Photograph by Oberto Gili
166–171. Roger Wade/*Architectural Digest* © 1997 Condé Nast Publications, Inc. Reprinted by permission. All Rights Reserved.
172–177. William Waldron/*House & Garden* © 1998 Condé Nast Publications, Inc. Reprinted by permission. All Rights Reserved.
178–183. Laura Resen
184–185. Jacques Dirand/The Interior Archive
186. (top) © JRabinowitz Photography (.com); (bottom) Jacques Dirand/The Interior Archive
187. Jacques Dirand/The Interior Archive
188–197. Photography by John M. Hall, courtesy of *Veranda* magazine.
198–201. Michael J. Lee
202–207. Carmel Brantley, Brantley Photography.
208–209. Courtesy of Durston Saylor Photography and Fairfax and Sammons Architects.
210–211. Carmel Brantley, Brantley Photography.
212–217. Gordon Beall/*Architectural Digest* © 2003 Condé Nast Publications, Inc. Reprinted by permission. All Rights Reserved.